A BRAVE DOG NAMED
SHERLOCK

Paul Osborne is a fire investigation officer who has been with the Fire Brigade for over 20 years. In 2013, Paul was selected to be a hydrocarbon dog handler, one of just 14 teams across the country. He was paired up with the bright-eyed Cocker Spaniel called Sherlock, to help make London a safer city.

Sherlock is a five-year-old Cocker Spaniel with a nose for sniffing out ignitable liquids. He is very fond of tennis balls.

A BRAVE DOG NAMED
SHERLOCK

Paul Osborne

arrow books

1 3 5 7 9 10 8 6 4 2

Arrow Books
20 Vauxhall Bridge Road
London SW1V 2SA

Arrow Books is part of the Penguin Random House group of companies
whose addresses can be found at global.penguinrandomhouse.com.

Penguin
Random House
UK

First published by Century in 2018
First published in paperback by Arrow Books in 2019

www.penguin.co.uk

A CIP catalogue record for this book is available from the British Library.

ISBN 9781787460836

Printed and bound in Great Britain by Clays Ltd, Elcograf S.p.A.

MIX
Paper from
responsible sources
FSC® C018179

Penguin Random House is committed to a sustain-
able future for our business, our readers and our
planet. This book is made from Forest Stewardship
Council® certified paper.

*To the four most important women who complete my life, Mum,
Emma, Olivia and Kate. With you in my life the glass is
always half full – or twice as big as it needs to be! xx*

Contents

Foreword by

Dany Cotton,

Commissioner, London Fire Brigade

Everyone knows that owning a furry four-legged friend is good for you – it's life-enhancing. Dogs make us happier and healthier, and they put smiles on our faces.

When the London Fire Brigade introduced specialist fire investigation dogs in 2000, I was over the moon. I love dogs, but there was more to it than that. Our dogs help the Fire Investigation Team to make sure that the people who deliberately start fires are convicted. Watching our dogs sniffing out a fire is magical. Their keen noses are more accurate than the most sensitive technology that has yet been designed to detect lightable substances.

Sherlock – that little bundle of energy – is a Cocker Spaniel whose official job title is Specialist Fire Investigation Dog. He joined London's ranks in 2013 and he's impressive. When you pass him in the street he might look like a normal dog; however, he's anything but. He's an integral part of London's firefighting and prevention team, helping us to keep the public safe. His drive is unrelenting and the speed at which he can track down an inflammable liquid has reduced the time it takes us to investigate the scene of a fire. His nose can home in accurately on even the faintest traces of something suspicious up to a year after it's gone.

But Sherlock would be lost without his committed handler, Paul Osborne. The pair really are a close-knit professional team, whether on or off the fire ground. Paul has twenty-one years' experience in the Fire Brigade. After honing his skills with Kent Fire and Rescue Service he came to London in 2005. He's been in our Fire Investigation department since 2009, hunting down the causes of fire, investigating fire scenes, and appearing in court to provide testimony in cases of fatal fire and arson.

I am delighted that Paul is sharing with us the wonderful story of his journey with Sherlock. We are so proud to have them as part of the London Fire Brigade team.

Dany Cotton
London Fire Commissioner

Chapter 1

D for 'Dog' Day

'Paul, you're going to be great in this new role, there's no doubt about that, but a little word to the wise: you won't know exactly what you're taking on with this job until your dog arrives. Remember that.'

At the time it seemed an odd thing to say for my mate and fellow Fire Investigator Mick Boyle. I wasn't exactly sure what he meant but as someone who was an experienced handler on the team and had looked after both Fire Dogs, Roscoe and Murphy, I trusted he had a point to make. We had enjoyed a fair few chats between shifts, lots of joking and mucking around over numerous cups of coffee. I took it as just some well-meaning advice from a well-respected colleague with a keen sense of humour, but this time there didn't seem to be a punchline – or perhaps I had missed it? To be honest, I was probably only half concentrating on anything anyone said because at the time my mind was focused on one thing and one thing only.

I was ready for this. This was what I had wanted for a very long time: my own Fire Investigation Dog – or, to be accurate, Hydrocarbon Detection Dog. Mick knew that being a handler would be my dream come true. And so Friday 12 July 2013 was D-Day – that's D for 'Dog'-Day – a day I will never forget. I was about to welcome Sherlock into my life. Sherlock was not just a Fire Dog; this fire-cracker of a Cocker Spaniel was the pride of the London Fire Brigade Investigation Team no less. He was seen by all my peers as the top dog: Sherlock was simply the best and he was about to be mine.

Was I up to it? More importantly, would Sherlock think I was up to it? Because if he didn't then we were all in trouble. It was one of those mirror moments, you know the kind? The ones where you take a good look at yourself and check behind your eyes to see if you're still in there? 'Mirror, mirror on the wall: who am I? What have I achieved? Where am I going?' Get the drift?

Let's start with what should be the easy one ...

Who am I? I am Paul Osborne and for the past five years I have been a Fire Investigator with the London Fire Brigade, with over twenty years' experience as a firefighter. I've seen some horrific things: sights that have made my own hair curl, and some I've had to tell myself to forget.

What have I achieved? I have a beautiful wife, Kate, and two gorgeous daughters, Emma and Olivia. All three are my greatest and proudest achievements and the source of my deepest joy. We live in a lovely house in Kent, my home county, that I'm gradually renovating with my own two hands. It will be perfect ... one day. That's what I've promised, so it will happen.

I heard the dog van draw up outside my house and a rush of excitement washed over me. It was a bit like that childhood memory of waking up on Christmas morning hoping Father Christmas had delivered that one special present you had been wishing for all year. It must be Sherlock. This was it.

If Mick had been on his own, he would have been knocking at the door by now. Bang ... there went the driver's door. The creak of the van's back doors opening that followed was a sound I recognised straight away. Then some kind of scuffle and rattle as something was taken out of the back ... The double doors slammed shut ... one ... two. Knock! Knock!

I was in my work wear – dark blue trousers and shirt with red LFB insignia – and I remember walking from the kitchen through the hall towards the front door, straightening myself up, making sure that I was all tucked in, as if Sherlock was going to conduct an inspection or be disappointed at how I looked. Daft, I know, but first impressions count even if you're meeting a dog – right? I opened the door and there was Mick with one featheryfooted crinkly-eared black Cocker Spaniel, one lead and one pink duvet.

'Here he is and he's all yours, squire. The best of British to you, and remember what I said – this is it now. This is when you begin to discover what the job is all about.'

Enter Sherlock. Or, as I've come to know him, Mr Bustle Britches, Sherlockster Rockster, or simply Rockster. Imagine, if you can, a chunky, furry ball of power-packed chaos suddenly landing in your living room and you have a tiny glimpse at the impact he made on us that morning. Sherlock hit the ground running ... through every downstairs room in the house and then out into the garden. He was on the sniff – this time, most likely, for food. My two daughters were still very young: Olivia was three years old and Emma was just past her first birthday. They were a bit too young to realise what was going on but the big smiles on their little faces said it all – their new playmate had arrived!

Sherlock was in top gear and I now know that when that happens, oh boy! There's no stopping him. This dog was on a mission.

His wiggly backside and crazily swishing tail seemed to have a mind and drive all of their own, knocking anything in their path crashing to the ground – including little Emma who was bumped by Sherlock's bottom as he hurtled past her and out into the garden. She was absolutely fine, bounced well and was back on her feet in seconds, full of giggles.

'No, Sherlock!' were probably the first words I spoke to my new work partner that day. His rear end was weaving frantically from side to side like one of those toy slinky dogs – you know the ones, with the section of springs between the head and the tail? Crash, bang … dig! Followed by more digging and, I'm reminded, lots of pooing too.

I stood with Kate and the girls and we watched Sherlock say hello to his new home – our home – and make his presence felt in my recently created flowerbeds. Thanks, mate! We gave him plenty of time to show himself around our place before showing him his own 'granny flat' at the bottom of the garden. He's a working dog and is used to having his own accommodation but I still hoped that he would like his special home-from-home cosy kennel provided by the Brigade.

I called him over to me and he walked beside me down the garden path to the desirable little doggy des res. Originally on the site of an old timber potting shed with climbing roses over the roof, Sherlock's new kennel was warm, spacious and the latest in design: it was insulated for the winter and had the bonus of a stable door for ventilation in the summer. 'Welcome to your new home, mate. What do you think?' Sherlock sniffed the bedding and the bowls and approved the collection of tennis balls (his favourite) and toys all specially selected for him with a good nudge of his whiskery, cream-speckled muzzle ... and then dashed back out into the garden for another good long dig through to the earth's core – via my flowerbeds!

'Sherlock, don't do that!'

That afternoon Kate decided that the best thing I could do was take Sherlock for a walk. Introduce him to his new haunts and the smells of the neighbourhood, that kind of thing, and I had a feeling it would be best to agree. We are very lucky to have a house that backs on to a beautiful park where there's plenty of room for dogs to enjoy being dogs and let off steam. In my head this is where I'd already planned to take Sherlock for his morning run before work and his last of the day. Needless to say, the park would become a familiar feature in his new life with me, so what better place to go on his first day? I collected Sherlock's lead from the cupboard in the hall and called him to me.

Now where had he gone? Just seconds ago he was right beside me. I walked back through the house to the garden expecting to find him nose-deep in my flowerbeds, but he wasn't there either. According to Kate she'd seen a Sherlock-shaped blur scooting back to his new kennel, which is where I found him sitting with his head bowed.

'What's the matter with you, silly dog? I'm trying to take you for a walk.' I reached towards him and hitched him up to the lead but that only made him dip closer to the ground. What on earth was wrong? I took the lead off and grabbed one of the chew treats that we had put in his welcome pack. If all else fails, food will not, especially with a spaniel. 'Come on then, mate, let's be having you.'

The chew treat got me as far as the front gate where I tried with the lead again but at this point I could see what the problem was – Sherlock, it seemed, didn't like the traffic. Not one bit. The noise and the rush of the vehicles clearly bothered him, but I had a feeling that if I could keep him distracted with tasty treats and some encouraging words over the 400 metres to the park then

7

we would be home and dry. 'That's it Sherlock ... good boy ... nearly there now, mate ... nearly there ...'

We made it to the park entrance and when Sherlock saw the open green space his whole demeanour changed back to how he was when he first arrived at the house – that bundle of bustle and sniff. As soon as his feet touched the grass he raised his head and that whole bum-wiggling thing restarted, and, with one look of approval from me, he dashed off to explore his new stomping ground. Sherlock was happy now, there was no hiding it.

I took a deep breath in as I watched him from a distance, pleased with the fact that the run in the park was such a big hit. He loved it! With acres of space to dash about, this was going to be a good place for us both to prepare for the day ahead or wind down after a busy shift. This felt good. Lost in my thoughts, pondering how wonderful the next phase in my career was going to be with Sherlock at my side, I was reminded that keeping a good lookout on what my new partner was up to was probably a good idea.

A flash of black fuzz caught my eye and woke me from my daydream. Had he found something? What on earth was he doing kneeling down under that tree? I could see other walkers taking an interest in what was going on, so I moved a bit closer to the shady spot where Sherlock had found a damp, grassy patch for himself. He was down on his elbows nuzzling into the ground – like a pig! What did he think he was doing? Digging for truffles?

'Hey, mate, is that your dog? What's he found over there, buried treasure? If he has I'm in for a cut!' A fellow dog walker couldn't help commenting and I could understand why. There was Sherlock, the pride of the London Fire Brigade, digging a dirty great hole – mud up his nose, in his mouth and plastered all up his forelegs. Grunting and snorting his way through the earth with a crazed look in his eyes and splats of dirt flying up in the air at all angles.

'Yes, he's my dog all right,' I found myself announcing proudly to the passer-by, but if there was no treasure in that hole I wondered if Sherlock was more likely looking for his brain! He looked so pleased with himself, his entire face peppered with splodges of earth and his big brown eyes almost spinning with sheer joy.

It was time to go, before the crater Sherlock was digging got any deeper and he attracted a bigger crowd. 'Here! Come on, you crazy thing. Let's get you home.'

He came to me right away and we strolled back towards the park entrance where I put him on his lead for the short walk down the street to the house. His head lowered; the sound of the traffic had already started to grab his attention.

'Don't worry, mate, we'll get this cracked. I'm not sure what's going on with you, but I'll have a chat with Dave and Clive who both knew you as a puppy and we'll sort something out.' But in the meantime, I made a mental note that we had to be careful next to traffic. Maybe he had been spooked by traffic early on and never got over it? Maybe we'd never know.

'There you go, you're home.' Lead off. And Sherlock's tail started to wag from side to side, taking his whole body with it. He looked like a dog settling in and getting comfortable. I hoped that was true. I saw Olivia's and Emma's reactions when Sherlock reappeared in the hall, and it was pure magic. The smiles on my girls' faces is a vision I will never forget. We had a dog in the house and there was no better feeling.

Fortunately, Sherlock had managed to dry out and shake off his muddy layer before we reached the front door. That's one of the many great things about spaniels – their self-cleaning coat. Someone must have put great thought into that when they were designed. After all, a dog that can dig that hard and get so dirty would otherwise end up spending 90 per cent of their time outside or in the bath. As it was, Sherlock emerged with just a few tell-tale clods of mud stuck in his beard. But that was all. I managed to knock those clean out with a stroke of my hand before

Kate saw a thing. I could see how a haircut would make things easier, not just for Sherlock but for me as his handler. I'd have to look into that very soon. For now I needed to give the lad some food.

I decided that he should have his supper in his new 'apartment' as it would help him get into his routine. When Sherlock was first acquired by the Brigade, he lived with a fellow investigator and dog handler called Dave Arnold. He was allowed to stay in the house, where he made himself very comfortable as a house guest, happily chewing his way through a selection of things including rugs, furniture, clothing and a pair of much-loved, and clearly tasty, flip-flops that he found and fancied. Hearing tales of Sherlock's destructive streak was one of the reasons why we gave him his own quarters, but also because Sherlock is a working dog it's less confusing to give him his own space rather than keeping him inside as you would a pet. Plus, our home wasn't anywhere near Sherlock-proofed, though that job had just jumped to the top of my home improvements to-do list.

That night Sherlock decided on his own bedtime. We noticed that he had disappeared to his kennel and when I went to check on him he was snuggled into the pink duvet that had arrived with him. I had added it to the rest of his bedding so that he had a familiar smell to sleep with on his first night with us. We don't really know how dogs feel when they experience a change of circumstances, but I think we can safely assume that having something they are used to alongside them is as important as a favourite toy or comforter is to a child.

I didn't want to disturb Sherlock, but I needed to check that he had his tennis balls and his toys to keep him occupied, so that he wouldn't howl the night away, upsetting himself (and the neighbours!). I wasn't entirely successful in tiptoeing past him undetected, but he was too tired to do more than check me out with one sleepy eye, slop his chops and rest his chin on his paws. I think I heard the first snore before I had secured the stable door for the night.

As I walked back towards the house I wondered again what that thing about hating traffic was all about, but perhaps it would turn out to be a positive – at least I knew he wouldn't run towards it when were on the job. We had also just made it through our first test of trust together: the trust that was going to form the basis of my belief in him as a Fire Dog and his trust in me as his handler. I felt for him, I genuinely did. But it was also something that I knew we'd probably have to manage every day. Only time would tell.

What my dog couldn't yet know (but would learn in our time together) is that I'm not a person to underestimate the power of feeling insecure. We all have our little demons that pop up when we feel vulnerable: when there's a new job to learn, new people to get to know, new challenges to define our strengths and test our weaknesses. They are the things that make us who we are. I was sure we would work it out together.

It had been quite a day for everyone and we had all played our part to ease Sherlock into his new life, and I had the feeling that it was only the start of a voyage of discovery for all of us – not just for Sherlock and me.

Kate was in the kitchen fixing a drink for us to relax with in the garden. I went upstairs to check on the girls, expecting them to be fast asleep, but Olivia was wide awake and bursting to ask me about Sherlock. She wanted to know if he was comfy in his bed and if I'd wished him sweet dreams. He had been with us for less than twenty-four hours and Sherlock was already part of the all-important night-time routine. I assured her that Sherlock was all tucked up in bed and was bound to have sweet dreams after such a great day.

As Kate and I sat surveying the devastation that our new family member had inflicted on the garden that day, I asked her if she had wished Sherlock sweet dreams too. She said she was glad that at least when he was asleep he was still! Everything that was on his level and on his flight path through the house had been relocated to save it from harm: ornaments, lamps; anything decorative or delicate was in danger of being bumped or swept away by his tail or his lump of a rear end.

So that was our first day with the lad himself. We had stood and watched while Sherlock dug up the garden that I had worked so hard on. The raised flowerbeds were now lowered, or, more accurately, scattered, and there had been a lot of clearing-up to do in the doggy-toilet department. But in all other ways it had been a good day and was stacked with positive signs that Fire Dog Sherlock was feeling happy and relaxed in his new home.

My family learnt a few lessons that day, the most important of which was that Sherlock has only one speed and that's 'top speed'. And don't be fooled by the 'butter wouldn't melt' act either. He knows what he wants and where he's going to get it. If it's food, then nothing will stop him. Nor will he let anything stand between him and his beloved tennis ball. Sherlock's drive was and still is unrelenting. It's what you want to see in a working dog, but in one like Sherlock it's still there when he's off duty too.

Kate and I stayed up later than usual that evening and our entire conversation centred on Sherlock, but that was bound to happen given his momentous arrival. We talked about how handsome he is and how his colouring resembles a bar of rich dark chocolate with white chocolate swirls running through all the glossiness, landing in patches here and there. There are speckles of cream on his feet – the front left paw has the biggest splodge – and there's more on his muzzle and chest. It's as if he has been painted by someone who has difficulty staying within the lines.

And then there's his beard, which gives him the impression of wisdom beyond his years – except when he drools in it and the slobber goes everywhere. His sleek ebony body is stocky and muscular yet so perfectly proportioned. His cute little face, bright eyes and alert expression and droopy ears covered in wavy dark brown hair are offset by a curly topknot, that in summer turns a strange shade of burgundy.

Both Kate and I had dogs when we were growing up and our families still have dogs now. If I'm honest, I always wanted a spaniel but never had the space to give over to such an energetic breed. I think the attraction is that you never really see a sane spaniel. They all seem to be a bit bonkers, and wide-eyed with an air of mischief about them. It's as if anything crazy could happen in their company and I like that. Their need for lots of exercise and their tendency to be a little unhinged didn't faze me in the slightest, but all that drive, inquisitiveness and focus needs an outlet so I can see why they make such amazing working dogs. Now, thanks to Sherlock, all of that massive spaniel personality was going to be part of my life.

Kate and I laughed, remembering parts of the day, and how Sherlock resembled Taz the Tasmanian Devil cartoon character. 'It's the way he whirls into a room, spins around, creates mayhem and spins out again. He just can't sit still, can he? It's crazy, but I guess that's who he is; we'll just have to get used to it. After all, it's Sherlock all over, isn't it?' I said to Kate, who looked at me as if to say: 'That had to be a rhetorical question.'

'Paul, I don't know why you think I'm not already used to living with a Sherlock-type whirlwind. Surely you can see how similar you two are? You are so well matched because neither of you can sit still for a second. You'll get on fine together, there's no doubt about that. And me? Well, I think Sherlock must be baby number three, or maybe our first challenging teenager!'

This woman had known me since we were at school together; she had been married to me, and therefore to the Fire Service, for nearly a decade. Clearly, she knew me better than I knew myself. But I had Kate's support, and that meant everything to me. I had brought the dog-handler role into my everyday working life which was no small undertaking, but I had also brought the dog into my family life. If Kate didn't mind having me and a four-legged version of me around the house, well, I couldn't ask for more.

In the quiet and darkness at the end of that first day, Mick's words echoed in my head. It dawned on me what he meant when he'd said that I couldn't know what the job of a dog handler entailed until the dog arrived. The future was starting to take shape for all of us, and as I told myself that to make this job a success I had to make it work with the rest of my life, I imagined Sherlock saying: 'Ah … home!'

Chapter 2

A Very Special Kind of Dog

Ever since the fateful day that Sherlock burst into our lives, I've often wondered whether he has an off switch. He never stops moving. When we're working – or on a shout as we say in the Brigade – Sherlock and I could be actively searching for hours on end, and his energy reserves will never seem to dip; he'll still be bounding around, raring to go again, whilst I'll be in desperate need of a coffee. So whenever we finish a job, there's always one place we have to go: the park. I'll have a look on a map to see if we are close to somewhere I can give the old boy a good run and just let him be a dog for a bit. And if there's a coffee stand for me to grab a take-out, then all the better.

Wherever we go, Sherlock is my priority. He's not the kind of dog you can 'park' while you collect your drink from inside a café. There's no way I would like the job of explaining to our Commissioner, Dany Cotton, that I had 'mislaid' Sherlock. I'm sure my ears would be ringing louder than all the fire bells in the country if that ever came to pass. I'm well aware that the skills of the Fire Dogs are well known and respected within the Brigade and when you see the value a dog brings to a fire-investigation scene it's understandable. It's no shaggy-dog story – dogs like Sherlock are worth more than their weight in gold and are as important as any other member of the team.

It was obvious from the beginning how precious Sherlock was going to be to the Brigade. Even before he started his training, his pedigree said everything about his potential. If there's such a thing as a *Who's Who* of working-dog dynasties, then Sherlock's family tree would take up several chapters. He came from good championship stock where the retrieving instinct had popped up time and time again. The drive and instinct to sniff things out was in Sherlock's genes.

Clive Gregory, the man responsible for pioneering the use of Fire Dogs with the London Fire Brigade, has, in my opinion, another claim to fame, because it was Clive who was responsible for acquiring Sherlock. Almost every time we meet Clive says that his one regret in life is not taking Sherlock's brother as well. Clive knew that he had a puppy packed with potential, but when he saw how Sherlock developed into a dog that didn't just have the drive and intelligence needed to do the job but had an almost sixth sense too, he could only imagine that Sherlock's brother, the one remaining pup in the litter, would have been the same.

There's no doubt about it, Sherlock was a handsome puppy, and Dave never tired of telling me as he regaled us with stories of what the little ball of fur was up to whilst he was looking after him. But it didn't take long for Sherlock to prove to everyone that he was not just a pretty face. He was five months old when Clive decided that the Brigade's new charge was ready to be tried out. He didn't want to push him too soon, but Sherlock was showing a maturity that's seldom seen in a dog so young and he was always looking for things to do. That energy needed a focus that didn't involve chewing furniture!

His first test needed to be a bit of a challenge but not so great a challenge that it might overwhelm him and turn him off. With his knowledge of training Fire Dogs, Clive had already decided that if Sherlock didn't find the scent he had laid down or even show interest in what was going on then nothing was lost: he would just rest him, and try him again later. There was nothing to lose but everything to gain if the new dog was ready to start training in earnest.

Whenever I hear Clive utter the word 'jaw-dropping' I know that he is talking about Sherlock. It's an expression that trips from the lips of anyone who's seen Sherlock in action, even in those early days. The first test that Clive decided to set for the pup was to hide a test sample of ignitable fluid in the stores, amongst the stock of uniforms, and then introduce him to the room. Without a second's hesitation, Sherlock bustled in and settled to the search, nose to the ground, then in the air, sniffing hard and then … he froze.

Clive froze too! This was more than a puppy indicating an area of interest; this was Sherlock with a full-on positive indication, and he took just seconds to locate the test sample. This was the eureka moment that Clive and Dave were waiting for. They say it was *the* moment that they knew that Sherlock was going to be an exceptional trainee Fire Dog. What Clive Gregory doesn't know about dogs isn't worth knowing, so Sherlock was definitely the dog to watch.

As weeks went by I got used to hearing Dave talk about Sherlock and his funny little ways. I remember being in stitches as Dave recounted how a child's sock went missing, which is not a big concern for most parents because we all know there is a massive black hole full of socks somewhere out there in the ether, but if you have a puppy in the house a missing sock is a potential gut blockage, and this sock had disappeared without trace. Dave decided there was only one place it could be: inside Sherlock. They had looked everywhere else, and as 99 per cent of other missing objects had ended up in the same place, there was a huge possibility that the sock had ended up there too. It was just taking more than the usual amount of time to pass through his system. Poor Dave and his family were on 'sock watch' for several days before, as predicted, it eventually 'reappeared'! And as for Sherlock? He just carried on as normal without a care in the world, totally unaware that eating that tiny sock could have killed him.

I was very fond of Dave so when he announced that he was retiring from his job as a Fire Investigator I knew I was going to miss his camaraderie. What I didn't know was that this decision would herald a life change for me too. Dave's main Fire Dog, a yellow Labrador named Sam, after many years of dutiful service, was due to retire to a life of leisure with the family while Dave took up a new position within the Brigade. This left two vacancies available. Sherlock was going to fill one of them, but who would get the handler job? I had to go for it.

I had been a Fire Investigator for two years, but I was now the closest I had ever been to realising my dream of adding Fire Dog handler to my role. And knowing that whoever got the job also got Sherlock was a real incentive. I wanted this so much I could taste it.

Applying for the job was just the start of a very long process, and in the weeks that it took to go through each stage I had my heart in my throat most of the time. And my inner voice was working overtime: was I ticking all the boxes and giving myself the best chance of getting this job? Well, the most important thing was that I love dogs and had them throughout childhood, so I knew the practical side of how to look after a dog. I didn't see a problem on that front. I was established in my job and I considered myself experienced enough: nothing was popping up as a total surprise to me these days. So that was a good sign. I also lived in the area covered by the London Fire Brigade so there would be no problems with deployment to whenever and wherever I was required. But that wasn't the end of it.

I will always remember our family holiday to France that year, not because we were in what has to be one of the most beautiful parts of the world, but because it was dominated by my efforts to work through a lengthy reading list. Kate and the girls had to put up with me having my head in a book every time I came to a standstill, but everyone knew why I was doing it. I wanted this job and I could see how it would be not just a career move for me but a positive life change for all of us. I was worried that having a young family would work against me in my application, as the pressures of a Fire Investigator position plus a dog plus a young family could equal a whole lot of stress and anxiety. And in my darker moments, I couldn't help thinking, was I good enough? My journey into the fire service hadn't been an easy one, and my own personal demons from that time kept rising up in my mind, but all I could do was polish up on every requirement in the job spec and give everything in my power to the interview and presentation. I wanted everyone to see that this job had my name all over it, but at the end of the day it all came down to putting in the hard work and holding on tight to what my dad has always said to me: 'You can only do your best, son.'

I knew that the only thing that mattered was having a go, so as I sat soaking up the French sun, determined to be ready for the presentation, the interview and the dreaded test that were waiting for me when I got home.

And Sherlock? Well, by all accounts he wasn't wasting time doubting his abilities. Knowing him as I do now, he certainly wouldn't have been doing anything like the amount of navel-gazing I was! The buzz around the whole of the Brigade was that he was destined for greatness, but whenever I saw him he looked oblivious to his stardom. Even now when I'm working with him he blows me away with how accurate and quick he is on a search, but then I see him wandering about in the garden looking for something to destroy or sitting in the rain wearing a semi-gormless expression with his nose surfing the air, and I'm irresistibly reminded that in addition to being an amazing working dog he is also still … just a dog.

While I was living through the job-application process the closest I got to spending time with Sherlock was when Dave gave him his run in the yard at our base at Dowgate Fire Station. Sam (who we nicknamed 'Forrest' thanks to his uncanny resemblance to Forrest Gump) was there too, but you couldn't miss Sherlock: he was quite the scene-stealer even then. And, just like everyone else, I was guilty of honing in on the shiny new dog and made a point of visiting him in his kennel. 'How are you doing, mate? You all right? Who's a handsome lad then?' I stroked his little bearded muzzle and gave him a good rub behind his wavy ears. He seemed to like that, and I was delighted he responded to my voice. Just sitting with him made me immediately calmer and to my surprise he too was still as I chatted to him.

I had spent enough time with Clive, Mick and Dave and their dogs to see how strong the bond could be between dog and handler in this job, and it's very, very special. I loved it when Sherlock licked my hand, but I couldn't risk getting too attached. If I didn't get the job, then it would be game over. There could only be one thing worse than not getting the job and that was watching Sherlock working with someone else. I couldn't let that happen.

There was one final part of the application process for the dog handler job: David Robinson – the Station Manager at Dowgate Station and the man responsible for the London Fire Brigade's dogs – had to come and inspect my home. Being a Fire Investigator is a tough job as it is, but throw in a furry cannon ball and it can turn your life upside down if you let it. But that's not just for the handler themselves but for their families too. David was kind enough to visit Kate and the girls, to explain more about what it would mean if I got the job. 'You've got to be strong with this job, and I certainly don't want this to fail, but if Paul gets the job and you ever think he struggling, talk to me. My door is always open. Whatever happens, it's always something we can deal with, and he won't lose Sherlock. Just know we're here if you need us.' Having a dog in the family has a huge impact, and knowing that there was a support network there for all of us if we needed it was a huge comfort.

I can honestly say that I've never worked so hard for anything in my life as I did for the job to handle Sherlock. The powers that be didn't make it easy, but then it shouldn't be easy to get such a responsible position. At the end of it all, when David called me I was feeling slightly numb. I think

I had consciously put my head in a place where, whichever way the decision went, I would be able to respond to disappointment with an air of 'of course, great result, absolutely fine'. In reality, I was somewhere between practising my acceptance speech at the Oscars and preparing for the humiliation of a 'crash and burn'. (I always find those words from *Top Gun*, my favourite film of all time, will spin into my head whenever I'm feeling the pressure. I didn't feel much like Maverick that day, I can tell you!)

The call from David was short but very sweet: 'Paul, the job is yours. Well done.' I could have turned cartwheels. Maybe I did! The moment was a bit of a blur: I'd got the job and therefore Sherlock was coming home with me. It was definitely the high point of my career so far. I had made it. After soaking up some very kind words from everyone at the station I couldn't wait to tell Kate. I knew that she'd be happy for me; after all, she was the one who had seen the blood, sweat and tears that I'd put into getting this job. She was the one who knew exactly how much this success meant to me.

I remember calling Kate at work: 'I've got it! I've only gone and done it! Thank you for everything you've done to help me. I'm over the moon ...' I think I kept talking for quite a while, to the point where I wondered if Kate was still on the line! 'Are you still there?' I ventured.

'Yes, Paul, I'm still here. It's amazing news. But I have one question – when do we get the lovely Sherlock?'

That dog … I had to accept that my working life was no longer my own. From now on there would be no 'me'; it was all about 'us'. Sherlock was my partner, my fellow investigator – and do you know what? It felt good! The hard work had paid off; now the harder work was just about to begin.

Chapter 3

The Hard Work Begins

I'm not sure if I believe in the fates or in God but certainly if there were other powers at work at that time, no one could have been more pleased than me with how the stars swirled and aligned for me. David's announcement meant that Sherlock would be coming under my wing pretty quickly, at a time when we could both launch into a fresh working partnership under the watchful eye of Clive. I always credit Dave Arnold for heroically mentoring Sherlock through his destructive puppy stage, which saw the demise of several pairs of shoes and countless items of clothing. In truth I had loved hearing these tales of naughty puppy Sherlock and I think I fell for that daft dog a little bit more with every funny story I heard. What's more, there was always a sense of pride when Dave talked about Sherlock's antics. 'You'll never guess what Sherlock has gone and done now …'

Sherlock was our new recruit and, consequently, was afforded all the affection and ever-present pranks that go with the job. He belonged. He was one of us now, and his ballsy behaviour was only to be expected from a puppy bursting with energy and retriever instinct. Dave had his timings all worked out, including the bit where Sherlock needed a handler just as he was about to start his training in earnest.

In this job you have to get used to change. People may join, and then decide that the Fire Service is not for them and leave. Even if someone makes it their life's work and stays until they eventually retire, they can move to different stations or change jobs within the Service. Whatever happens, change inevitably affects the dynamics of the team, and it's the teamwork that makes things tick and work so well. Firefighters are all team players – they have to be, because out on a shout they rely on each other to stay alive. They attend a fire together, go in together, and look after each other. The investigators, and dogs like Sherlock, Roscoe, Sam and Murphy, play their part by identifying causes of the fire rather than locating casualties, but we are all pieces of the same jigsaw puzzle. And as the pieces move around, the team makes sure that all bases are covered.

Having said that, I knew the Brigade would miss Dave and his trusted sidekick, Sam. They shared a close bond and that would have made it difficult for Sam to pass to someone else. That's how it is with Fire Dogs: 'one person for one dog', something I understand far more now than I did back then. As for Sherlock? Well, I had the feeling that even though we were a newbie team in training, I would spend the early days learning more from him than he would from me!

It was all systems go now, and the new job and training routine started pretty much immediately. I knew that we were up against it as soon as I was told that, instead of the usual five-week block of training, Sherlock and I had to cram all we needed to learn into two weeks and three days! Unfortunately, we were in the mindset of the austerity cuts for the public services, so Clive, as our trainer, would have to pull out all the stops to get us through to graduation in double-quick time.

We made a plan: we broke down the allotted time into two- and three-day trips, giving Clive the chance to teach us something new that we could go away and practise before moving on to the next phase. It wasn't ideal, but it was about making it work for everyone. Although Sherlock wasn't officially on duty, I took him to work with me every day so that he could get a feel for what lay ahead. He went everywhere in the van with me, he got used to the sirens when we were responding to a shout, and of course I was driving faster than normal when we had to give it the blues and twos to cut through the traffic, but the speed didn't seem to bother him. It was all new to him, but Sherlock didn't turn a hair.

Our training sessions took place at Wethersfield air base in Essex, or sometimes at the Fire Service College in Moreton-in-Marsh, Gloucestershire, and under Clive's direction and guidance we worked through exercises to hone Sherlock's sniffing skills using samples of ignitable liquids and our search skills as a team. I was the one with the experience but, frankly, you wouldn't think so some-times. At some point in every session Sherlock would deliver one of those much-talked-about jaw-dropping moments. Clive had tested Sherlock from day one and every time he watched him very closely, not so much to see if he could locate the scent, because that was inevitable with this dog, but to record how quickly he could do it!

To be fair to Sherlock, he delivered amazing work every day of those first days together. If Clive set a test scent, Sherlock would find it. No messing. If I ever thought of myself as an experienced member of the Fire Service Sherlock would prove me wrong by teaching me something new and putting me right. This ten-month-old pup was an old head on young curly shoulders, and every time he looked back at me and gave me that 'in your own time, mate' look, I knew that he wasn't taking the mick. I felt that he was being very patient with me.

Clive had been testing Sherlock on and off for several weeks before I came on the scene, so Sherlock wasn't fazed when his sniffing samples were presented. I kept him on the lead for an exercise where we worked through a series of tins and bags to 'indicate on' but not 'interact with'. Each session we covered a different discipline with a good splodge of 'housework' – that's searching burnt-out buildings – thrown in. This is real bread-and-butter territory for us, and it's where I could help Sherlock get used to the larger search areas. My experience as an investigator really came into play here because if there was one thing I knew about, it was searching buildings. When we are called to a fire scene the property search often includes a distance of several hundred metres either side of the building as well as the entire floor space and the garden and outbuildings. Many commercial premises cover much larger areas and Sherlock needs to stay focused all the time. If it's a big job, we take several short breaks, so he can clear his nose and have some fuss from me to encourage him to carry on searching. And at the end of the entire operation, he is rewarded with his tennis ball. That's something that he learnt very quickly. As far as he's concerned, that's what this whole thing is about.

During our training I watched him all the time: how he moved and how he reacted when he indicated and all the other little signs. We were getting to know each other: me getting to know all his little quirks and him getting to know me and the inflections in my voice. We were figuring out what worked best for us, such as getting Sherlock to focus in the busy chaos of a fire scene by using our trigger words: 'Find the bomb.' We used this specifically because it's not a common phrase, so when Sherlock hears it, his ears prick up and he knows it's time to get down to business. Keeping Sherlock concentrating and making sure I could read his body language were all part of the training process. We were learning together, becoming a team; every day brought something new for me, and it had to be the same for Sherlock too. I made sure we paid maximum attention in Clive's classes, and under his expert guidance I felt that I was learning to read Sherlock a little better every day.

However, practice makes perfect and that's what Sherlock and I did. We would get up early and practise the scenarios Clive had put us through over and over again, whenever we could. We had to be ready and prepared before the next training session, we couldn't let Clive down. It also boosted our confidence, for Sherlock as a dog and me as his handler. We were quickly becoming a finely tuned unit. I could tell from the way Sherlock was paying so much attention to me, hanging on my every word, that we were growing closer.

Clive was as supportive as ever, and if I had anything I was unsure of or wanted to go over I would call him, or sometimes Mick, who was always happy to give me the benefit of almost a decade of experience doing this job.

As Sherlock was now with me 24/7, if I was on a case where an accelerant had definitely been used (sometimes the smell is a dead giveaway), I'd take him into the property to identify the spot where it had been introduced. It was useful practice for Sherlock, but it also gave me a chance to observe him and read his body language in an environment where I knew there was something for him to find. Every moment was a chance to practise.

I wanted him to learn to trust me, trust that I would never put him in a situation in which he was in danger or order him away from an area before he had completed his search to his satisfaction. That I would keep him safe and give him plenty of praise. And in return I would trust him to cover the ground how I wanted him to, trust that he wouldn't miss anything and would identify anything he found. One of the hardest lessons I had to learn and grow into was this: no matter how right I think I am, it's the dog who is always right!

Clive had instilled in me the importance of being a team and never shouting at my dog because we would be a single, bound unit. Not a man and a dog but one team with complete understanding of each other. So having Sherlock at home and around the family meant that he was always with me. Work and downtime, we were together. We inhabited the same space, mixed with the same people and spent every waking hour in each other's company. As we got to know each other, I soon learnt that wherever we went together there was a strong chance that he would outshine and upstage me just by being himself. And when it came to our graduation, he pulled out all the stops!

There was no doubt about it, the pressure was on and I never took it for granted that we would graduate purely on the merits of my brilliant dog, but I admit I was hoping that I wouldn't let him down. Clive was always ready to put us through our paces, and was equally happy to spend time watching Sherlock work. I'm not sure that after two weeks and three days of observing me he saw me as poetry in motion, but Sherlock? Well, that was a different matter.

Our graduation was essentially a dry run of the certification tests that we as a Fire Investigation Dog team have to do every year. Even with that knowledge, I can't say I wasn't nervous. Clive set five tests, through a series of six purpose-built burnt-out rooms – one could be a bedroom, another a taxi office. They are mocked up to mimic real-life scenes, so that we can use the skills we've learnt in our training in the sort of practical environment that Sherlock and I might come across in our work. Twenty-four hours before the test Clive spread twelve different combinations of ignitable liquids and solids over the test site. Some were diluted, others neat, evaporated or burnt, and it was then up to Sherlock to locate each one. In phase one, Sherlock was given free range to search off the lead, but in phase two I had to keep him on the lead while he took direction and guidance from me. This was our chance to show Clive how we worked as a team and Sherlock threw himself into it with his usual enthusiasm.

I was alongside Sherlock the whole time, and what he was showing on his graduation day was a real Hydrocarbon Detection Dog masterclass! This was it, I thought. The scenes were burnt out and the smell of charred wood and smoke was everywhere – they were incredibly authentic, but that didn't faze Sherlock. All that hard work and training meant that he was familiar with fire scenes and knew what they smelt like. Amongst other smells, there was petrol in the air; Sherlock picked up on it immediately but he had to pin it down amongst all the other scents filtering through his nose to the spot where it had been deposited. No problem. He caught the scent, then brought his nose down, then back up again. He was surfing the air with his snout, his head bobbing from side to side like Stevie Wonder at his piano. As always, his rump end was swishing from side to side too, with his tail like a little whip hitting a rhythm all of its own. He ran into the wind, letting it take him to and from the scent, and then back out again, up and down, up and down again, narrowing down the area. He was well on to it and then ... he got it!

He was just as impressive working on the lead. A row of canisters with holes in the top containing a range of aged accelerants (so fainter scents) got Sherlock's full attention. He pulled ahead to sniff each one in turn – his juicy black nose almost resting on the lids. He moved steadily between the cans, taking my direction to ensure none were missed, and he revisited any he had shown an interest in first time and wanted to check out again. And all of this in double-quick Sherlock-time. I was waiting to see it – the full-on Sherlock dance. That's the one that says: 'Got it, Dad!'

There he was, Sherlock, like a pint-sized weightlifter, his muscular legs and power-packed shoulders stomping on the spot and virtually waving at me with an outstretched paw: 'It's right here, Dad! I've found it … look!' Tongue lolling out of his mouth and eyes shining and shifting to meet mine – there's no mistake when Sherlock has a positive indication. There's a whole lot of snorting going on and I soon discovered that when the scent is very strong the poor lad sneezes. If we hadn't had Clive watching our every move I would have laughed out loud; I'm sure deep down Clive allowed himself a good chuckle. I knew we were being assessed, but to Sherlock this was just a great game and he was having huge fun working for that tennis ball.

It's always hard to hold back on that all-important tennis ball when Sherlock does so well. But it's the ultimate prize, and when there is more than one area to check it's up to me to make sure that he stays focused on the search to the end. Give him that tennis ball too soon and, as far as the dog's concerned, there's nothing else to work for. Job done! So I need to fill the gap. I tell him: 'You're a good boy … There's a clever dog. Well done, mate …' and there's lots of fussing and praising at each stage. Funny thing is, the look in Sherlock's eyes that he gives back to me says almost the same thing: 'You're doing great, Dad, but we've more work to do.' He always looks for the tennis ball, but if it doesn't come he carries on searching until he has finished and I say we're done. Then he has earned it. Yes, it's a game but it's an important game with a lot resting on our shoulders every time we are called to a search.

Finally, the paperwork was delivered and there it was in black and white: 100 per cent success. Sherlock had done it. We had done it. As I was writing up my paperwork, I wrote in the corner of the certificate 'GATW' – Good All the Way – as they say in the RAF. We had not just made it, we had smashed it! We had graduated from Clive's training with flying colours, and it felt so good.

I was so proud of that crazy dog. I've seen others at work and they are all impressive, they are all little characters, but Sherlock – he makes everything look so easy. He's just a blur of fur and I can well understand how some people might think: What on earth is that dog up to? He's all over the place! The thing is, he *is* all over the place to start with, because he wants to find the accelerants that he has been trained to find. He is full on and is taking everything in. And when he settles he *will* find what he's looking for – if it's there to be found at all.

Good communication, as in all relationships, is vital if a team is going to gel and progress. During our training and graduation, I found myself talking to Sherlock all the time. Now I talk to him at home, at work and when we have our 'us' time on walks. He knows my voice and I'm always calm with him. I promise I try to be calm even when he has totalled my latest bit of DIY in the garden or has sneaked something from the house and buried it. Sherlock can't speak to me and he can't understand the words I'm saying but the lilt and intonation of my voice has to say: 'Trust me,' just as much as my physical praise and play says: 'You're safe with me.'

No matter what I'm saying, he'll gaze at me with his velvet-brown eyes moving from side to side, so you get the dots of the white as he looks dead at you and then quickly away again in a kind of rapid eye movement. Then he starts to spin around on his back legs, like a hairy Sugar Plum Fairy, with his eyes still on me. It's pure concentrated excitement and obviously all he wants to know is: 'Where are we off to now, Dad? What's happening next?' That's all he's interested in because if I'm still in uniform he knows there's a chance that we'll be off in the van and he wants a part of the action. He's up for searching whatever I put in front of him. He wants to please me, which means he wants to do his job.

I see him as an extremely professional working dog, but I know that in addition to that he is also a dog who just wants to play. The game is to detect the presence of ignitable liquids, and he goes about this with extreme focus and drive. Even if he views his life as just an enjoyable series of meals, walks, trips in the van, things to sniff, things to bury, haircuts and sleep, to the rest of us he is a vital member of the team.

Chapter 4

It's All About Trust

'Trust your dog. Believe in him and he will lead you ...'

More wise words from my friend Mick Boyle that are etched into my brain. I am forever grateful for his calm reassurance right from the start. The echo of these words and many more have helped me every day since he first shared them with me over a cup of coffee early one morning when Sherlock and I were just starting out. 'If your dog says an ignitable liquid is there, then it is there. If he doesn't indicate but you think it's there – trust him that he's right and you are wrong.' Just five days after graduating with such aplomb, we attended our first deployment together and, oh boy, was Mick right.

The shout came through as a Firefighter Emergency, and believe me, for anyone who does this job, it's the last thing you want to hear. Two of our own had been injured in a potential arson attack and we were heading to Tottenham without knowing if our colleagues would survive.

The large Victorian property comprised of a ground-floor shop with several flats above and I was visualising the usual mix of flights of winding stairs, blind corners and narrow corridors for Sherlock to search. Images of the fire damage told me how big a job this was going to be and how large the area was we had to cover. It's one reason why I wasn't surprised to hear that Sherlock would be needed to search before excavation and again post-excavation – that's after the debris had been lifted off the ground.

I could tell that the police, fire crews and ambulance personnel on the scene were looking to me and Sherlock to come up with some answers as to what had started the fire and had put the firefighters' lives in danger. I already knew that we wouldn't have any magic answers; all we would be able to confirm was if there was an ignitable liquid present and where it was. I knew Sherlock would do that for them and that we could play our part here.

Everyone was all over this scene and already the Brigade had begun working with the latest technology: computer fire modelling. In this case, Sherlock and I would be helping to gather as much information about the scene as possible (e.g. the configuration of the building, its purpose, what was likely to be inside) to help the computer modelling software reconstruct the scene of the fire. Not only would this help the firefighters learn about what had happened, but it would also provide some much-needed answers for the families of those injured in the blaze. If Sherlock found traces of an ignitable liquid then it would provide vital information about what had caused the pattern, ferocity and the dynamics of the fire.

As a Fire Investigator I had my own questions: what series of events had culminated in fire gutting the property and two firefighters fighting for their lives? Why did the firefighters get into trouble at that point on the stairs and have to escape through the window because they thought they were going to die? What had happened?

We had to get this right.

I sensed the weight of responsibility from the moment we arrived on the scene, but now, all dressed in my protective white marshmallow Tyvek® suit, I was aware that I had a big job to do, and big boots to fill. If I could have spoken to Clive or Mick, they would have reminded me that it was OK to feel like this on the walk-through but once I had Sherlock with me on the search then I needed to jettison the pressure from others because it wasn't fair to pass that on to my dog. I had to remember what I had been taught: the dog handler is in charge. Only the dog's handler can say what the dog is allowed to do, and after that, the dog is always right.

I was ready. I walked with a fellow Fire Investigator beside me who shared vital information about what they knew so far and we discussed possible ways forward. My top priority was Sherlock's safety. Looking at the blackened shell of a building and the layers of ash and debris I could tell there was no chance that a human being was going to find any evidence with the naked eye. Everyone knew that if there was a chance of finding anything that afternoon the most useful tool would be Sherlock's nose.

As I stepped beyond the police tape and entered what was left of the shop section of the building, I stared around and tried to imagine what had been there only a few hours before. The fire had run and raged fiercely so it was no surprise that we were walking through broken glass, chunks of masonry and heat-twisted metal, and everywhere at ground level there were shelves of ash and splintered wood that stood out to me as danger zones for Sherlock, who could slip under them as he searched. I scanned the scene room by room, taking in signs of anything that looked as if it didn't belong or was misplaced, that could provide a clue or be useful to have Sherlock check out later. Was it

safe enough for him to walk through with me at his side?
I went to get him from the van.

'Come on, you, you've got to earn your money now.
You can't sit in the van all day so how about you do
some work?' I remember feeling jealous of him because
it was so cold outside. Sherlock doesn't feel the cold, but
I needed to put an extra fleece on under my fire gear.
'Oh, by the way, Rockster, it's a bit of a mess in there so
you'll have to wear your boots.' As I was talking to him
I reached for a set of four dog boots and started putting
them on Sherlock, who clearly wished I wouldn't bother.
He had worn them several times before but reluctantly,
and protested by walking very weirdly as if someone had
tied pillows on his paws. I couldn't risk taking him in there
without protection because I could feel the heat in the
ground, and the chances of him stepping on an invisible
nail or tack were high. This time he was more patient with
me and sat perfectly still while I put the little Velcro-tabbed
bootees over his feet. He plonked about in them for a bit,
but we still had to do our little walk from the van to the
scene of the fire, so he would have a couple of hundred
metres to get used to his footwear.

'Now, Sherlock, you're going to have to take this one
steady, mate … No rushing through, since you're likely to
find some soft spots under your feet. But don't worry, I'll

be right with you. And I'll warn you now, there's plenty of eyes going to be on your every move and every sniff, so remember all you've learnt and give it your best – and I promise I'll do the same.'

We booked in with the duty officer and stepped through the police tape. At every major incident, firefighters are required to book in their named rider boards with command control. This is so that we know who is covering the scene, but also, should there be a firefighter emergency, the rider boards are used for head count. Everyone there that day was all too aware that the two men who hadn't responded to their names were battling for their lives in hospital. Now all eyes were definitely upon us.

I was inside, trying to focus and remain calm. I took a deep breath and knelt to speak to Sherlock, who was sitting at my feet, shaking with anticipation. 'So, you're going to find something, aren't you? You're a good dog.' I said these words clearly, which he knows as 'working words' and bounced his tennis ball to remind him of the prize. Then our trigger words: 'Find the bomb ...' and off he went. He set off at fifty miles an hour but soon slowed to a good steady pace as his nose lifted to sift the smells in the tight hall space. He swaggered on through, getting used to the feel of the boots, and then turned back to an area of interest on a stretch of roofing felt. I noted it for the police, but it would be up to them if they wanted to bag the section for lab analysis. I could tell by the purpose in his body language and his enthusiastic snorting that Sherlock's senses were heightened. I talked to him all the while: 'Good boy ... you've found something ... clever lad.'

Then we moved through to the carnage in the shop area. The ceiling was down, there was glass everywhere, and the metal racking had virtually melted. This was a challenging scene for Sherlock and a much larger space than he had searched before.

We took breaks after every fifteen minutes of searching to give Sherlock's nose a rest as there was so much for him to take in. It was just a precaution on my part, because my dog was working methodically. I was careful to make sure that all the areas were covered, which meant some were checked twice. I didn't mind Sherlock looking over his shoulder at me, as though to say: 'But I've already done that bit, Dad ... There's still nothing there – just like the first time.' However, when he came to the ice-cream cabinet his body language changed. It was like the first time I saw him give a strong indication – he did one of his little dances and then froze. I knew exactly what he was telling me, and I remember thinking: What an amazing dog. I signalled to the Scene of Crimes Officer (SOCO) that Sherlock had found something in the debris beside the freezer, and when I heard the words 'Mark it up' it said everything about my dog doing his job well.

'Who's a clever dog? You're so clever ...' I praised him and then just had to give him a big cuddle before setting him back on the search. 'You're going to find it for me, aren't you, clever dog?' I couldn't help feeling a little bit guilty when he looked for his ball as the prize, but give him the ball and it's all over. Give him a cuddle and he will keep searching for me. As much as I wanted to reward him with the ball I couldn't just yet as I did't fully know if what he'd hit on was a target substance. In training it's different, because I know what he's looking for, so I know when he's due his reward, but in a real-life scene, where so much is at stake, we simply don't know. We can't risk rewarding our dogs on something that may cause them to falsely indicate; therefore when we're on a shout he won't be rewarded until I'm happy the search is completely finished. Instead, I kept my voice soft with a tone of suspense and encouragement, which must have been almost hypnotic for Sherlock because he carried on, totally keyed in to me.

I remember feeling overwhelmed at the fact that just under a week ago we had been diligently practising but now Sherlock was actually doing the job he was meant to do. This was very much the real thing.

Our search continued, and I knew that we were working our way up to the point where the firefighter crew had hit trouble. This was where my own demons came into play. As I was watching Sherlock cover the space I imagined what could have happened and thought about how the firefighters were lucky to have made an escape from the bathroom window on the first-floor landing – but only after the fire had overtaken them. If an ignitable fluid had been used in this incident it would have boosted the explosive energy of the fire, which could be life-ending. The temperature would have risen rapidly around the firefighters, and the room would have suddenly turned orange as the fuel in the atmosphere became fire above their heads, in what we in the Fire Service call a flashover. This is where the heat of fire radiating from its origin raises the temperature of all the contents of the oxygen-rich room, until they reach their ignition temperature, whereupon they spontaneously combust. The flashover meeting the sweating firefighters, despite being in full kit, would have created a boil-in-a-bag effect. The steam would have caused horrific burns, I was in no doubt about that.

I had this in my head as Sherlock searched. I could almost hear their screams – but I couldn't allow myself to go there.

We left no stone unturned, no crust of ash or charred timber or pile of dust either. Sherlock was thorough in his search, and by the time we clocked off in the evening I was able to alert the police to several areas of interest that Sherlock had detected in the property. From the floor next to the freezer in the shop, to what had been a sofa on the third floor, to clothing and discarded cloths. And the misplaced can of lighter fuel his keen nose found in the thick debris on the shop floor. Nothing unusual in that, except that the shop didn't stock that brand, which could prove to be a huge clue for the police to pursue.

Sherlock and I continued searching the wider scene, checking out the service road to the shops as well as the building's courtyard. I decided to take Sherlock down a nearby alleyway – the kind that the criminal would run down if this were a film. It was far enough away from the scene that I doubted there was anything to find, but little did I know that Sherlock, all wagging tail and snorting like a trooper, would search and find a brazier at the bottom and indicate on that! 'Well done, Sherlock!'

We all knew this was going to be a major operation – we needed answers, and with the added knowledge of our colleagues in hospital beds we all felt extra pressure to deliver good work. The next stage of our investigation was to excavate the scene, and the following day, once this was done, Sherlock and I went in again, helping to piece together the fire scene along with our colleagues in Fire Investigation and the Scenes of Crimes Officers over two full days. It was an intricate business and we couldn't miss anything.

As we worked the scene, I couldn't help wondering if this would turn out to be a case of Arson with Intent to Endanger Life or the lesser Reckless Arson. Both carry a heavy sentence but if there was a loss of life this would be even more. I looked to the sky and hoped that all our work would result in Sherlock's indications translating into forensic evidence which would bring a perpetrator to justice, and not a means of closure for the family of one of our own.

It would take weeks to gather all the evidence together but those two days searching the scene took it out of me. At the end of the day we made it back to the van and Sherlock had his beloved tennis ball firmly in his mouth. 'Don't worry, mate, I'm not going to take it off you. You've earned that ball today and then some. You can keep it with you, because if there's a park around here that's where we're going.' He looked at me as if he understood every word I said and agreed that sounded like a great idea. Probably my best of the day.

The reaction of the police officers on site was enough to make any dog handler burst with pride. When we arrived, we had been under pressure to perform, but I thought I'd overcome that and had managed expectations. We were there to confirm whether there were traces of an accelerant on the site or not. All we could promise was that if there was something, Sherlock would find it. And that's exactly what he did. I sensed some relief amongst the Criminal Investigation Department (CID) officers, and I understood that because as a result of Sherlock's work they had something to move on. And I liked being asked if they could give Sherlock a pat and a good ear scratch for his trouble. That's the power of a dog. Dogs bring everyone on to the same level and I'm sure they make better human beings of us all.

Although I was exhausted, both physically and emotionally, Sherlock still had energy that he needed to run off so I had a look at the map. I found a park for him somewhere and although I can't recall where, I do remember that I needed a walk as much as Sherlock did. My head was buzzing with what had taken place that day. Sherlock would go and dig, and I would wander behind him to keep a close eye on my teammate, just in case he decided to go walkabout. I'm not sure why I was thinking along those lines back then, but maybe it was because of the tough day that I didn't want anything to happen to him. I needn't have worried: even from his early days he showed that while he likes the people we meet in the park, he's only interested in digging. It's his waggiest and happiest self, and I knew that he would never run off.

Sherlock's and my job on this scene meant that we were the boots (and paws) on the ground investigating the incident. We had done all we could. Sherlock's day was over, and now it was down to the police to follow up. There is so much information to gather from a fire this size and it can be incredibly frustrating when we have to wait to hear the outcome as the police take over and the investigation continues without us. Sometimes it can take months, even years, for cases to come to court, and sometimes the results of an investigation never make it back to us. It's always an incredibly tense wait no matter how long it takes, not only for the families of those who have been injured, but in this instance for their wider firefighter family as well. It can be months of not knowing – but the sense of relief was immense when we later found out that the two firefighters were going to be OK.

I was sure it would take a good while for all the events of the past two days sink in, to take stock, but I appreciated how far Sherlock and I had come along. I now had a pretty good idea what I had taken on with this job, and this was just the start. Mick was right, it's not clear what the job is all about until you get the dog – and what a dog Sherlock proved to be from day one. We had arrived. This was absolutely it. I called Sherlock over from whatever hole he'd been digging, packed him in the back of the van, and, exhausted, we drove home.

'Sherlock? What are you doing out there? You can be more intelligent than that, mate. You really can …' I was standing looking out of the kitchen window and wondering what on earth my dog was up to. There he was with a state-of-the-art heated kennel just a few feet behind him, and he'd chosen to sit in the rain – in the middle of my once very lovely but now very flattened oriental grasses.

'Kate, come and look at this.' My wife was getting used to being called to witness Sherlock's latest daft moment. 'That is supposed to be an intelligent dog. Just hours ago, he was stunning the police and the forensic teams with his skills, and there he is, the brains of the outfit, sitting in the garden in the rain when he could be inside in the warm. Crazy animal!'

I put on my boots. I can't leave him out there casting such a lonely figure in the rain, I thought. OK, I know he'd be fine, because he's a dog and his thick black coat has an oily texture, a bit like an otter, so the water just runs off his back and drips off his ears, but what on earth was he playing at?

'He looks happy. Maybe he's just relaxing and letting the day out of his head?' Perhaps Kate was right. 'You have us and your DIY and exercise regimes and all that to help you unwind – oh, and what's left of the garden. Maybe this is just his little bit of Sherlock-time.'

I'm not sure if Sherlock knew that we were watching him or if he could hear us, but just as Kate finished speaking he got up, gave himself a massive shakedown and skipped off into his kennel.

'I'll just go and have a word with the old lad and dry him off. It was a tough day today.'

Chapter 5

A Hard Day at Work

'Paul, we have a fatality for you and we need Sherlock
along too. And by the way ... the body is in situ and
it's not a pretty sight.'

It's not unusual to start our Watch eating breakfast and
looking at images of a fire scene, which is also the last
resting place of a person, or persons, consumed by flames.
I could say it's something you get used to, but I'm not
sure that's true.

I had been working with Sherlock for just five months
when we were called to our first fatality. As a Fire
Investigator I have attended hundreds of searches where
property has been damaged and sometimes people have
been injured, but every time a search involves a loss of

life it feels like the first time because, in my job, the only thing fatalities have in common is the presence of fire. In every other respect each one is unique.

When the bells went down in the early hours of that morning, the police and a London Fire Brigade crew attended the scene in New Malden along with two of my fellow investigators. As my day always starts with walking Sherlock it was wasn't surprising that I was in the park when I got the call to say that we were both needed on this, our first call-out of the day. From the conversation I gathered that it still wasn't clear how the fire had started, so the team at the scene needed our help: if Sherlock detected traces of an accelerant, or confirmed there was no accelerant present, it would help narrow the possibilities.

As it was a handover case I wasn't going to be the lead investigator this time, but the need for Sherlock's skills had, for now, put us at the forefront of the initial investigation.

Over breakfast I was briefed in full. This was what we knew so far: a figure was seen running, in a ball of flames, down a street and over a level crossing. Footage from security CCTV cameras captured the person's last moments before they fell, still burning, on to a grass verge. There were reports of someone following but at that time we had no evidence of that. And it was hard evidence that the police SOCOs and CID needed, and, as always, they needed it as soon as possible.

While I was getting up to speed, Sherlock was making his rounds. It turns out that the rest of White Watch (the team of firefighters who I work with) are a pretty generous lot when it comes to a cute spaniel wearing a pathetic, wide-eyed, sad expression. Even the toughest, burliest firefighter finds Sherlock's 'I'm starving because my dad doesn't feed me' look impossible to resist.

'All right, you, that's enough of that, clever dog ... Let's go!' I have to pull him away – it's my way of saying to my colleagues: 'Please don't spoil my dog; he'll be as fat as a bucket if we're not careful!' I love Sherlock, he's my mate, but as a working dog he's a very valuable piece of fire brigade 'kit'. As a Fire Investigation canine team, we're on call 24/7, 365 days a year, so wherever we find ourselves and whoever we're with, he's fit and my respon-sibility and I need to make sure that he's ready for duty. If we're needed then we must be there; we rest, but we don't really rest. It's that kind of job.

I didn't need to get Sherlock into his harness because he had arrived 'in uniform' so, in theory, all I had to do was round him up. I say that, wishing it was always that easy. For some reason, Sherlock has no problem getting in the dog van or the works car at home or when we're out on a shout, but as soon as he gets wind that we're leaving the station he goes on his own mini walkabout or stops to 'chat' to whoever happens to be around, and generally pulls out all the delaying tactics in his dog book to avoid getting in the van.

There's usually the ritual dancing around a bit with whoever he has found at the station to be his friend. Then there will be the head-bobbing and tail-wagging combo, before he realises that there's only one end to his performance – he has to get in the van! Imagine, if you will, a boxer throwing a few punches at an invisible opponent before stepping in the ring ... that's Sherlock wiggling about before he realises. I'm not missing about. This lasts just a few moments, but the impatient side of me still finds it slightly annoying. However, really it's just another one of Sherlock's many little quirks.

'Come on, you daft dog. Let's go and do a day's work, shall we? And don't think for one second that you're going to get your chops around any of those doughnuts I saw on the table. Believe me, you can think again, mate!' I lifted him into the kennel section in the back of the van where he settled down straight away – as he always does.

We had a forty-minute journey ahead of us from our base at Dowgate Fire Station and I hoped that would be more than enough time to process the grisly images that were starting to loop through my head. The brief provided enough detail for me to visualise what we'd be facing when we got there. It's at times like these that I almost envy Sherlock's ability to adopt a 'business as usual' approach to every fire scene. He has no preconceptions: he meets every job with a fresh attitude and a clear nose. He doesn't know if he's going to a burning building, a smouldering car, a gutted factory or, as in this case, a charred body. He can't make anything out of images put up on a screen and he can't interpret the words of a colleague giving their first-hand account – that's for me to process and make sense of. All Sherlock needs is his nose and his instinctive drive to locate what he has been trained to sniff out.

I knew for sure that if there were traces of an accelerant to be found in this case then Sherlock would find them, I trusted my dog's skills and therefore his ability to help the police take the investigation to the next stage.

As I approached the area I saw what I expected – the scene had been preserved, with roadblocks put in place and the railway line and level crossing closed to traffic. It's vital that Sherlock is given the chance to search before the scene is disturbed in any way, and that includes human footfall. The sight of the blue-and-white tent that is placed over the victim's body always makes my heart thud a little bit harder. It was Sherlock's first fatality, but I had seen all of this countless times before. Years as a firefighter made sure of that. But, as I said, it's not something you get used to.

The trick is not to let it get personal. But that's easier said than done.

You see, as Fire Investigators we are looking to work out what really happened at the scene of a fire: how the fire was started, who might be involved, was it deliberate? In the case of a fatality, it's part of the process to gather clues about the deceased's life, because something in that could provide information that might explain the lead-up to their death. Where they lived, who lived with them, the company they kept, what was precious to them ... all nuggets of information or pieces of the jigsaw puzzle.

Whatever could lead to someone's life ending in a ball of flames on a roadside?

I pulled up about 200 metres from the blue-and-white tape the police had used to cordon off the scene. It was a crisp December morning and, as I stepped out of the van, my boots crunched on the frost-covered road. Sherlock would have to be patient for a while longer as I had to go ahead of him to conduct a risk assessment of the search area, to make sure it was safe for him to be there. I was looking for broken glass, exposed cables, poisons for vermin, unstable floors or walls, that kind of thing.

I collected sealed packs containing a white Tyvek® suit and overshoes, plus a pair of green Nitrile gloves from the stack in the back of the van and started getting kitted out. I pulled the white forensic-approved suit up over my normal workwear and made my way towards the police officer who was booking everyone in. Watch Manager Osborne and Fire Dog Sherlock. I gave our my names and our roles on the investigation, knowing that I could be hanging around there for ages and that it would probably be several hours before we were able to book out. But that's the case for everyone there – you stay until the job is done. The forensic approach and the paperwork is all good practice and maintains continuity for the police investigation and for the Crown Prosecution Service (CPS), should the case reach court.

I was told that the victim was a young woman who was known to the police. She had been placed in a halfway house for her own safety, and it was from there that she had been running. It had been reported that she was alight when she left the house, so we had our probable place of origin and that was to be our starting point.

The building itself didn't appear to have been touched by the fire, and walking through the house there wasn't much to see, and there wasn't a great deal in the way of belongings either. Pretty much what you would expect for someone living in temporary accommodation: scattered clothes, toiletries, shoes and carrier bags. The room itself wasn't charred in any way, so despite the victim being seen running from the house, my first thought was that the ignition hadn't taken place inside the building as originally suspected – but that doesn't mean we wouldn't search the property anyway. It would only take an extra five minutes, but the evidence we can gather from extending our search is so much more. There may be nothing, but there might just be something – a footprint laced with accelerant, or a bottle cap perhaps? Things that you might not notice in the chaos of a fire scene, but Sherlock's nose would find in an instant.

After going over the whole building, it didn't take me long to decide that there was nothing in the house that would endanger Sherlock while he searched, so it was time to bring him in. I made my way back to the van and guess who was pleased to see me. Sherlock was sitting up, tongue out, ears forward, his wiggly bottom already swaying with anticipation. There was no need to grab his boots for this job. He didn't need his feet protecting from the heat or debris on the floor – not this time. I knew that he would be pleased about that because he was already stamping his feet ready to go and get on. I attached his lead and we headed off.

Our search started away from the building where the victim ran from. Beginning at a distance of 800–1,000 metres from the cordon, we covered the surrounding area – known as the overlap – before gradually working past the blue-and-white tent and back towards the property. I always want Sherlock's nose to be clear and fresh on the scene, so walking him in is a good idea. Sherlock, like all Fire Investigation Dogs, has been trained to detect all common ignitable liquids and solids, including petrol, paraffin, white spirit, turpentine substitute, diesel, cellulose thinners, lighter fluid, barbecue fluid, acetone and methylated spirit. Sherlock's highly sensitive nose hones in on any traces of his target materials, including the smallest sample, and even when the fluid is long gone. His nose is so powerful that he will indicate on any ignitable liquids or solids he can find, so this could range from naturally occurring substances in a scene, such as the acetone in nail-polish remover, or suspicious ignitable materials such as lighter fluid found on a doormat. The presence of an accelerant doesn't necessarily mean foul play, but Sherlock's indications help build the story around a fire incident and provide vital evidence. Whatever Sherlock finds, it means questions need to be asked. I wasn't expecting him to find anything on the way – but you can never really be sure. I leave that to Sherlock. If he does make any indications, then it means we have a trace of accelerant on the route, which the police could find interesting.

We approached the address of the suspected origin of the fire and Sherlock was happily bounding around, nose in the air searching for even the faintest of scents. Suddenly, on the pavement outside the property, Sherlock's body language changed. He crouched down low, nose to the ground, indicating on a blister pack of pills discarded on the path. 'Look what I've found, Dad. Over here, look!'

The police SOCO and the Homicide team were gathered around the scene, and all eyes were on me and Sherlock. A young woman had died in a horrible, violent way, and everyone was eager to find out what had happened. Any finds that Sherlock indicated on were potentially very important for investigation, as the police could decide that it suggested someone else was involved in her death, and they would want to be on that person's tail as soon as possible.

I flagged the blister pack of pills with the SOCO and Sherlock bustled back into action, giving the entrance and hallway through to the victim's room a thorough sweep-over. He slowed down as I directed him back towards areas that I thought he had skimmed over, but he was right first time. There was nothing there. No area of interest to report. We processed the whole house without any indications for his target substances.

As we worked through the property we went to check out the back garden. Sherlock got very excited and locked on to a mattress believed to have been moved from the deceased's room and that had been discarded in the garden. Two areas of interest, extremely valuable to the SOCOs because, to them, there were no visible signs of an accelerant – but Sherlock's nose found it right away.

Sherlock's job was done. In the fifteen to twenty minutes it had taken for the road search and to cover the address he had narrowed the field of possibility for the forensic team. Despite the team's initial thoughts on arrival at the incident that the fire had started in the victim's room, Sherlock's nose alongside other evidence from the scene, had told us otherwise. The forensic team were able to take samples of the accelerant from the exact spots where Sherlock had shown interest, and lab tests would then identify the type of ignitable fluid or solid present, meaning the investigation team would have the valuable evidence they needed to take the investigation further.

We were all aware that someone had lost their daughter, and maybe sister, aunt and cousin, that cold December morning. The victim was also a young mother. So many lives changed in an instant.

When I had completed my duties as Fire Investigator and Sherlock's handler on site we were free to book out and make our way back to the dog van. It was 200 metres of thought and reflection. We had done our bit and now it was over to the forensic team, the lab technicians and the police to take it further. The blue-and-white tent had been dismantled as it was no longer required. The road closure would remain for some time while local inquiries continued, but for everyone else life went on – as it always does.

I was so proud of Sherlock. I had attended many similar scenes before, but this was the first time since we graduated that I truly felt aware that I was no longer working on my own. In the intense atmosphere that surrounds a fatality, especially when the life lost is so young, having a dog on the scene can be very comforting: on a work level, a Fire Investigation Dog is an efficient and reliable member of the team, but he offers more than that. On a more personal level he is a great source of emotional support too. It's not unusual to see even the most experienced police officer or hardened firefighter reach out their hand for the comfort of Sherlock's warmth and attention. Sherlock's not just a valued colleague, but your best mate too.

Chapter 6

What's in a Name …?

I've heard it said by someone, somewhere, that if you give a child an impressive or unusual name then it will inspire them to live up to it. The international film and music scene glitters with stars burdened with strange, bordering on stupid, names so maybe there is something in the whole idea. Take Sherlock, for example.

I think Sherlock is a great name for a Fire Investigation Dog. In fact, I think, like the dog himself, it's perfect. I'd say that 99 per cent of people asked to name a great British detective would say, without hesitation, Sherlock Holmes. Even people who've never read any of Arthur Conan Doyle's books or seen any of the films or the many television series about the Victorian super-sleuth and his faithful sidekick Dr John Watson will know the name Sherlock

Holmes. But I have one criticism of the name as one for a dog, it's that it can't be shortened, which means I'm always yelling 'Sherlock! Sherlock!' – which is OK, but it does get folk chuckling when I'm calling him in the park. They often come up to me to tell me it's funny, and it *is* funny ... That is, until I explain what he does for a living and then the name is suddenly not so much amusing as impressive and considered spot-on for a dog who spends every working day as a scent sleuth.

From a slightly selfish perspective I've skipped around the entire name thing by developing a double-whistle as a recall device. It works well for me especially when we're out and about, but it doesn't stop other people's inevitable impulses to give Sherlock a nickname.

When Mick was working his dogs, Murphy and Roscoe, the lads had it easy. Murphy was 'Murph' and Roscoe was 'Ross' and everyone was happy that they had a nick-name and that was that. Sherlock made it a bit more of a challenge. So what did my Watch mate Mark come up with? 'Fluffy'! And do you know what? Sherlock still answers to it!

Looking at Sherlock now, with his military-style short back and sides, it's difficult to see where the name Fluffy came from, but back then he had the fluffiest coat on the planet. He really was a fluff-ball, with all the usual spaniel traits of feathery legs and feet, a fan-like tail and was very hairy, so, in the end, I guess Fluffy made sense at the time. The thing was, we had become full-time hard-working members of the Fire Brigade, and for very practical reasons I needed to get Sherlock a haircut – and fast. First of all, when he had long hair and he got wet, anyone who was within striking distance of him shaking down was wet too. Come rain or shine, Sherlock is a digger and a water-baby, so unless you like getting yourself and your vehicle covered in mud, a shorter coat had to be the way to go. And there was something else: I needed to be fully aware of my dog's body language while we were working so I could see how he moved and learn to read those movements during a search. Without the long hair everything was going to be easier and more practical for the job.

There's one thing about dog walking in the park: it's a great way to meet people, and Sherlock can be a bit of a crowd-puller. He's not over-keen on approaches from other dogs and usually sorts out the pecking order very swiftly so he can get back to digging a hole or scratching up grass, but the owners of the dogs that Sherlock rejects are never offended, so at some point we end up chatting, and one of the people I met, a lovely woman called Debs, happened to mention that she is a dog groomer. The timing was perfect, so I wasted no time booking Sherlock in for his transformation.

Of course, I had no idea how he would behave in a grooming parlour and I have to admit that I was apprehensive. Sherlock and I had only just become acquainted really, and he was something of an unknown quantity in social situations. As a partner detecting crime he was as solid and dependable as they come, but socially he was still an unfolding story. He was good around my colleagues at the station, and even now when Mark calls him Fluffy he will happily dance away from me with an air of 'Who are you? I've got friends ... don't worry about me, I'm busy with my mates ...' but in the outside world he still keeps himself to himself and his eyes on me. I don't mind that; understandably, it's because he wants to be wherever I am – because that's when it gets exciting! But at the grooming parlour ... ?

The day of the haircut arrived, and I reminded Debs that Sherlock was a first-timer and if he misbehaved then I was already truly sorry and would never bring him again. But I could tell from her patient expression that she had heard all of this before and I was likely the only one of us with concerns, because she was absolutely fine. I remember rattling on about this and that and what he was like and what he didn't like and then, as I drew breath, she good-naturedly said it might be best if I left and came back later because, from what she could see, Sherlock was going to take this whole haircut experience in his stride.

I went as far as waiting outside the room but didn't get myself too comfortable in case I was called in to sort Sherlock out and calm him down. I was convinced that the buzzing of the trimmer would be a problem even if the click of the clippers hadn't bothered him. To me there was a whole host of things that could go horribly wrong.

I heard the trimmers, the water, the splashing and then an hour later ... there was Sherlock. He looked as if he had shrunk in the wash. There was definitely less of him, but he was looking very handsome, and he shone like a piece of sea coal. Despite all my worries Sherlock had proven to be the perfect salon client: he sat and stood still as required, didn't complain or throw a strop or anything, but he did look a little confused by his new hairstyle!

I had asked for his feet to be left semi-feathery and for his ears to be spared the trimmer. I love his little hairdo on top which, as it was summer, had the auburn blush, so I wanted that left alone too. But the rest of him, including his now close-shorn tail, was looking good. He resembled a kid about to start 'big school' but without the baggy blazer. 'Well, hello, Sherlock! So is that what you look like under all that hair! Thanks for being a good boy and not letting me down in there.' I gave him a good old pat on his new curly-as-a-lamb coat. 'I can't wait to get you down to the station – now let's hear them call you Fluffy!'

Sherlock was in uniform. He had shed the 'clothes' that could have defined him as a pet dog. He was now, without doubt, a smart working dog, and after a couple of hours he let go of the kind of embarrassed expression that might be worn by a nudist at a church fete and started to groom himself in all the usual doggy places. He went about it as if he needed to check that everything else was still there! He looked for his tail, it was still there, he licked his paws, still there, and then he gave a twirl as if to say: 'I could live with this new look.' It must have felt so different for him, but he looked and smelled much better. He had a sartorial elegance about him – just like his literary namesake.

We were only just around the corner from home and I couldn't wait to hear what Kate thought about Sherlock's new look. He had less hair to shed around the house, so surely that was going to be a plus point. 'Look who I've brought home!' I announced in the hall. 'Have you seen this dog before?'

Kate was impressed, giving our newly preened dog a bit of fuss, but she was busy too, and as *Strictly Come Dancing* was on later she was keen to get the girls sorted out and some nibbles ready for us to enjoy while our meal was cooking. Sherlock was calm to the point of looking a bit subdued, so I decided to let him stay in the house with us for a while. He didn't seem to want to destroy anything, and he was quick to pick up his tennis ball in the kitchen, so he had something in his mouth, which usually means that he's a happy bunny.

I was keeping half an eye on him and I remember feeling relieved that he was being a good boy. Perhaps the new haircut had had some kind of Samson effect on him and sapped him of some of his bravado? Anyhow, he was happy, so the evening progressed. We moved away from the telly and the snacks to have our meal, but when we returned to the lounge, something was missing.

'Paul, we didn't eat all the olives and bread earlier, did we? If we didn't eat it and we didn't take it away – where is it? Paul … where's Sherlock?'

I had already learnt to cringe when I heard those words. Where was Sherlock? Good question.

I heard a lot of quick tapping and scratching on the wooden floor and then an odd rustling sound that I couldn't identify. Then I caught a glimpse of Sherlock nipping through to the kitchen. I headed into the lounge where I nearly trod on the remnants of the bread, olives and nibbly bits that we had stupidly left, at Sherlock height, on the coffee table. The oily tray and spat-out snacks had been shoved under the corner of the sofa. It wasn't going to need Mr Holmes to deduce who had helped himself to our food!

Chapter 7

A Little Bit of History

Despite his naughty antics meaning he may not always live up to the reputation of his fictional namesake, Sherlock's name isn't his only link with history. In a way, as part of the modern London Fire Brigade he is busy making history himself. The LFB's Fire Investigation Dogs are pretty much at the cutting edge of a service that has been saving lives in and around the capital since 1866.

The formation of the Brigade as we know it today has roots that stretch back to the Great Fire of London in 1666, when thousands of people lost their homes and businesses as flames consumed street after street of joined-up timber buildings. Londoners decided that the only way they could stop the fire spreading so rapidly from one property to another was to demolish buildings in its path and break the chain. The mammoth fire and the frenzied approach to putting it out was an experience that no one wanted to repeat. The lessons learnt went on to influence how London could be rebuilt with fire prevention in mind, and the ad-hoc arrangements for putting out fires transformed into small, organised fire services.

It's no surprise that those services were under the direction of insurance companies. After all, they were the ones with a vested interest in property and its protection. Other small independent firefighter units were set up all around the city, but they weren't acting in a joined-up fashion until the formation of the London Fire Engine Establishment under the leadership of James Braidwood. Braidwood was the brains behind the first municipal fire brigade in Edinburgh, which was manned by uniformed officers who were also the first to wear any kind of protective gear. The London branch had eighty firefighters and thirteen fire stations, but it was still funded by insurance companies.

Sadly, it took several massive fires, including the Palace of Westminster in 1834 and the Tooley Street Fire, in which Braidwood lost his life, in 1861, to stir up the insurance firms, who then lobbied the government to provide and manage a co-ordinated fire service in London. Four years later the Metropolitan Fire Brigade Act was passed and the Metropolitan Fire Brigade formed on 1 January 1866, but it took until 1904 for it to be called the London Fire Brigade. For the next thirty-five years everything ticked along fine until the outbreak of the Second World War, when everything changed again. If there was a time that London and other major towns and cities throughout the country needed a fire service, it was then. Nightly raids by swarms of German bombers were wreaking havoc up and down the country and turning the skies red with fire. All over Britain hundreds of small local fire brigades were drawn together to deal with the national crisis under the umbrella title the National Fire Service. Three years later, in 1948, the separate London Fire Brigade for the County of London was re-established, and later the formation of the Greater London Brigade expanded its reach even further so had the capital covered as never before.

The London Fire Brigade has been keeping its promise to make London a safer city for over 150 years and in 2000 it introduced a new and innovative piece of kit: the first ever Fire Investigation Dog. Handled by Watch Manager Pat Lyon, the black Labrador called Odin attracted a great deal of attention – and scepticism. Could a dog be a detective?

The idea of using detector dogs to confirm the use of accelerants in fires was first introduced in the USA in the mid-1980s and was picked up in the UK by the

West Midlands Fire Service (WMFS) in 1990. Sadly, the dogs didn't get the go-ahead at that point but there were still enough people in the system who believed in the idea to wait for the right time and opportunity to try again. That chance arrived in 1995, when the then chief officer of the WMFS, Graham Meldrum, later to become Sir Graham Meldrum, HM Chief Inspector of Fire Services, decided to introduce Fire Investigation Dogs into his brigade.

This is when Clive Gregory first appeared on the scene. Clive, then a specialist Fire Investigator, was selected as the project leader and handler due to his lifelong association with dogs and his dedication to the original research in 1990. In 1996, Clive and his specially trained dog, Star, became the first operational Fire Investigation Dog/Handler Team in the UK and members of the WMFS Fire Research and Investigation Department.

Clive and Star were an overnight fire-service success and quickly and convincingly overcame any remaining sceptics. As a team, dog and handler pioneered the use of Fire Investigation Dogs in the fire services of Great Britain and Northern Ireland.

In 2000, the London Fire Brigade invited Clive and Star to demonstrate their skills to a full meeting of the Brigade's Fire Committee. The Committee was so impressed that the document approving the implementation of their first Fire Investigation Dog/Handler Team was signed that same day. Television appearances on *London Today* and *London Tonight* attracted plenty of attention and won the initiative further support and approval within the Brigade and beyond.

Success followed success, and by 2004 the London Fire Brigade management were ready to approve an expansion, which would provide four teams, one to be available to each Watch (Blue, White, Red and Green) giving twenty-four-hour cover. Each dog was to be handled by a specialist Fire Investigator. Clive, who was a fully qualified trainer by this time, was selected to oversee the training of all four teams and maintain their operational capability with a structured maintenance and advancement programme. The first recruits, Star and Odin, were soon joined by Roscoe (and Mick) and Sam (and Dave). These trailblazers were later followed by Murphy in 2012 and Sherlock soon after.

This development within the Fire Brigade was recognition indeed for the dogs, recognition that would only grow. I was a leading firefighter based at Dartford Fire Station in September 2001 when the 9/11 terrorist attack at the World Trade Center took place. The mood was grim and there was a definite air of 'there but for the grace of God go I,' which extended into our families too. It was not a good time, especially as it dominated the news for so long; for anyone involved in the Emergency Services in particular, it was, to say the least, unsettling. Every image of giant New York fire rigs lying crushed in the burning pile at Ground Zero sent chills down my spine. The people were just doing their job, but that day they didn't come home. The New York Fire Department lost 343 souls as a result of the attack and all we could do was reach out with messages of condolence. That didn't feel enough. But what it did mean was that the UK powers were desperate for us to be ready in the unfortunate event that we were next. Given the extreme and devastating nature of the attack, we felt the probability of that happening rise 1,000 per cent.

Just four years later, on Thursday 7 July 2005, London faced its most deadly attack since the London Blitz. Four suicide bombers carried out a co-ordinated attack on the London Underground, which affected lines into Aldgate, Edgware Road and Russell Square. A red double-decker bus full of passengers was also targeted at Tavistock Square. The bombers, intent on causing maximum carnage, caused the loss of fifty-two lives that morning, and 784 people suffered life-changing injuries. The attack stretched the resources of the police, ambulance service and the Fire Brigade – I was one of the members who attended the scene.

And there were others on duty that day, unseen by most people, but who carried out valuable searches for secondary explosive devices and to clear safe passage for the emergency vehicles to reach the casualties: dogs. Arms and Explosives Search Dogs from the City of London, British Transport and Metropolitan Police were working to detect potential threats and offer reassurance at each of the affected locations.

Just as the work of the search dogs at Ground Zero in the aftermath of 9/11 highlighted the value of their work in other parts of the world too, the 7/7 bombings in London had a similar effect in the UK. Previously unsung canine heroes serving with the military and the Emergency Services were, at last, receiving some deserved recognition. The attention of the media also helped attract welcome funding for a number of search-and-rescue organisations. With these Service Dogs at last in the spotlight it was no wonder that when members of the public see a dog in harness being handled by a man or woman in uniform they now assume one of two things: the dog is carrying out some form of search-and-rescue operation or that it might be a cadaver dog trained to locate the dead.

Meanwhile, the Fire Dogs were still going silently and diligently about their duties – famously in the shadows.

My colleague Mick often tells the story of the time he attended the scene of a fire with Roscoe and couldn't help noticing a man hanging around but not speaking to anyone. As Mick gathered himself and Roscoe to go back to the van the man found his courage and stepped forward to ask a question: 'What does your dog do then?'

Having decades of experience under his belt, Mick had already done a mental profile of the man and labelled him trouble. 'My dog? This dog here?' he said, pointing to Roscoe. 'Well, my dog here catches people who set fire to places like that!' The man was clearly struck dumb and sheepishly shuffled away. It was no surprise to Mick that the guy was later picked up for questioning in the case. It was suspected arson with the use of an accelerant – thanks to evidence Roscoe detected at the scene. That's one way to be educated about the role of Fire Investigation Dogs!

Although dogs like Sherlock are a relatively new tool in the Brigade's box of equipment, they are favoured over the techno choice: the Gastec. This clever piece of tech takes samples from the air and analyses the particles to assess whether there are ignitable substances present. They're clever, but I'd go for the power of the dog's nose anytime. That's why the dogs have been used in many of our high-profile cases, such as the Cutty Sark fire in 2014, the Lakanal House fire in 2009 in which six people lost their lives, and at Grenfell Tower in June 2017. It's all about building blocks: building up the elements that can prove or disprove a case of suspected arson where accelerants are thought to have been used. It must be remembered it is just as positive for the investigation when an ignitable liquid or solid is *not* identified as much as when it is. This is because it allows the investigation team to progress with the information that they gain from having a dog search the scene. So often people look at no indication as being a failure, but this mindset is challenged daily by any deployment of the Fire Investigation Dogs: irrespective of whether a find is made or not, it shows how vital the dogs are as an asset.

Clive Gregory and Star. What Clive doesn't know about Fire Investigation Dogs isn't worth knowing.

Sherlock as a puppy – it didn't take long for him to prove that he wasn't just a pretty face.

D-Day – that's Dog Day. We soon discovered that Sherlock's greatest pleasure is to destroy tennis balls – we go through hundreds!

Our dogs are more than just amazing pieces of kit – they are our colleagues and our pals. (Mick Boyle with Murphy and Roscoe, and me with Sherlock).

Sherlock's new home – no expense spared for this dog.

Although Sherlock is a working dog, he is also one of the family.

Below: Sherlock knows it's time to get to work when he's got his uniform on. Here he's getting fitted for his harness by Sam at Jack Frost Pet and Country Store.

The little crimebuster getting down to work.

Right: When Sherlock's found something his body language completely changes. 'It's right here, Dad!'

Firefighters are team players – and Sherlock is afforded all the affection and pranks that go with the territory. Here Sherlock is brushing up the White Watch on some vital training…

Left: From the moment Sherlock came on the scene I had to accept that my working life was no longer my own. From now on there would be no 'me'; it was all about 'us'.

Sherlock's role is vital in helping solve crime. This is the clubhouse where Sherlock's discovery of **BBQ** gel helped to pin the source of the fire down to arson.

Getting out into the community is a priority for all 103 stations in the London Fire Brigade – and my partner is the best in the business for breaking down those barriers.

Left: Daisy Nimmo's dream was to meet and help train one of the Fire Dogs. It was amazing for Sherlock and me to be part of the team that made her dream come true. Here is Daisy with her mum, Stephanie. We gave Stephanie one of our tunics to wear, which Daisy loved.

Elementary, my dear Watson! Visiting Sherlock's namesake at 221B Baker Street.

Below: Peas in a pod – if you ask Kate, we're made of the same stuff.

Chapter 8

A Visit to the Vet

As talented as Sherlock proved himself to be, there was a time when I was worried we – the Brigade and I – might lose him.

Sherlock was about eighteen months old when I first noticed that he had a strange limp. It was a new thing – it had to be, otherwise I would have seen it before ... wouldn't I? When I say that it was a limp I could be more accurate and say that he had more of a 'funky chicken' movement with some head bobbing thrown in. It was more noticeable when he was running because he was thrown off centre. If he had been a car you might have said that it looked like his tracking was out.

I decided to have a word with Clive. My thought was that he had possibly seen something like this before and could give me some advice on what it might be. But then I guessed what Clive would say: it was obvious what I had to do. I made an appointment with the vet and kept my fingers crossed.

The finger-crossing thing must have worked because the vet couldn't find anything wrong with Sherlock's leg, but he did advise lots of rest over the next two months. Well, that was going to be the challenge of the century – keeping a mostly hyped-up working Cocker Spaniel quiet and off his legs. Good luck to me on that one! But I'd give it a try. Work was work and that had to be done, but the off-duty hours would have to be split between shorter walks and longer rests and keeping an eye on him in case he got any worse.

I was worried. What would happen if rest didn't work for him? Why had this suddenly happened? Clive had checked Sherlock's pedigree and there was nothing in his papers to suggest a potential problem. All his relatives had been A1 fit, so maybe he had done something to injure himself, or perhaps it was something we were still doing without realising.

I thought of our daily routine: the walk, breakfast, a day's work and then home again, with a walk at the end of the day. As I was pondering how I could adapt it for Sherlock's benefit I saw him sitting in the garden peeling one of his tennis balls – or maybe one of the neighbour's that had escaped over the fence – and getting all the green fuzzy bits stuck in his teeth and wisps of it on his whiskery chin. I walked over to him just to have a chat about things because he was really worrying me. 'I hope your leg isn't too bad, mate. I hope that kicking-out thing you do isn't hurting you, but I promise we'll get it sorted and you'll be all right. I really promise you that.' Then I left him to it. He loves to destroy a tennis ball; it's one of life's little pleasures for him.

Then I realised something: the tennis ball ... all the throwing in the park and Sherlock twisting and turning his body to catch it every time. Was there something in the repetitive, energetic tossing and catching that had done this? Well, it was time to find out – not knowing what was going to happen next was making it so much worse. I was afraid that my dream career was over, and Sherlock's too.

I took him to visit the chiropractor who confirmed that it was all the extreme movement to catch the ball that had caused it. It wasn't helping his recovery and we had clear instructions to adapt playtime. If that's what I had to do then I was going to do it, no worries. Except there was that word 'rest' again – how was I going to achieve it with a dog that is absolutely driven in his work and every move he makes is as energetic as the next? I knew I had to try. After all, he's my pal, I would do whatever it took to get him better. We were a unit and there was no way anything was happening to Sherlock. Not on my watch.

I listened to all the advice and put it into practice, but it was hard for a while because we all had to double-think everything to make sure Sherlock didn't overdo it while his back legs rested and the chiropractor did his work. Gradually, however, the leg kicked out less frequently and his body realigned with his head. It all came back together. One of the very few funny and lovely moments that we shared with Sherlock over that uncertain time was when he had an anaesthetic, and, for a while, it made him super-affectionate! He was cuddly in a way he isn't normally, which the girls just loved. The nice thing is that he has retained a little bit of that neediness, so now when he backs his rear end into me asking for some fuss I know that he really feels the need for some love and affection. He never has to ask me twice.

Those few weeks spent getting Sherlock back on his feet were a good bonding time. Of course we spend most of every day in each other's company, but during that period when I had to concentrate on reducing his exercise and making him rest when all he wanted to do was play, we talked *all* the time. Kate told me that I was even doing my 'Scooby-Doo' voice with him, which is a bit like high-pitched baby talk – something I never really did with the girls when they were babies, but I do it with my dog!

I'm not sure if this is true or just in my imagination, but I think we understood each other better after his injury. When Sherlock was back on full power I found we were using more sign language than words when we were on a search. It was as if my hands were magnetised: he followed them as if there was an invisible line between the two of us, and it was the same with our eye contact. The team was back, stronger than ever! And we needed to be, because we never know what's round the corner, or what challenges we're about to face.

Sherlock and I had been working together for a while when we worked another major case. This time it was a case of stalking that took an even more sinister turn when the stalker broke into the victim's home and lit a fire. I didn't get a chance to search the property with Sherlock initially because an arrest was made quickly after the incident, but when the police discovered that a kitchen knife was missing there were fears that the stalking victim was in danger, should the police be forced to release the suspect from custody. Time was of the essence and the police needed to cover all the bases, which meant they needed solid evidence – and fast. One outstanding query was whether the fire had been started with an ignitable liquid, and so I was invited to take Sherlock down to the police station to see if we could assist as the clock was ticking.

Was there any possible evidence that Sherlock could investigate? A search of the victim's home had drawn a blank, as had random items taken from the suspect. It appeared that everything intended for the lab was bagged and must remain bagged. But one item remained: the suspect's mobile phone. That was something Sherlock could investigate.

The phone was placed on a chair in a small room and the moment Sherlock entered his body language changed. He was giving it the full-on bum-wiggling thing but he also had a very determined stance – he knew something was there, but it wasn't at nose level. Suddenly he was up on his hind legs and standing like a meerkat looking at the mobile phone on the chair. He looked at me, then at the phone, and back to me … It was a positive indication. There was a contact trace of an ignitable liquid on the mobile and that was enough for the police to take away with them. But that wasn't all. Using the triangulation method of mobile-phone tracking, the phone could be placed at the scene of the crime. This was not just a high-five for Sherlock, it was a high-ten! The police had their man and the evidence to help prove it. This was Fire Investigation Dog work at its best.

I was over the moon with that outcome and was so proud of Sherlock. He really earned more than his tennis ball on that case. The police may have brought us in as a last resort, but that was OK because we knew that the next time those officers had a case where a Fire Dog might come in handy, we would get the call. The police want results and we provide them. That's one of the messages we are trying to get over to new CID entrants when we present to them during their time at the police training centre at Hendon. I love seeing the faces of the new recruits when they see Sherlock in action. They can't believe his speed and his accuracy, and they can't resist the chance to give him plenty of fuss. They will never forget how skilled he is and exactly what it is that Fire Investigation Dogs do.

Memorable cases come thick and fast when you work with a dog like Sherlock. The night we received a call for a blue light response to a car-showroom fire in Shepherd's Bush, I got the impression that Sherlock's keen nose was required to save the day. A high-end car dealership had gone up in flames, destroying several luxury vehicles and damaging many more, and the team on the ground were talking suspected arson. The request for the blues-and-twos approach meant that they were eager to get some plausible evidence in the bag, as soon as possible, while everything was still fresh on the ground.

It was pitch black when we arrived at the scene of the fire but looking at the size of the showroom it had been quite a blaze and certainly must have dominated the skyline for some time. There was some pressure on this case, but Sherlock being Sherlock was only going to take it at his pace, not the pace the police wanted him to. It was early in the morning and the good people of London hadn't yet left for the dreaded commuter rush hour so, with most still tucked up in bed, the chances of evidence being lost or displaced was greatly reduced. We always try to search a wider area for clues than the scene initially suggests, as we never know what we might find. Therefore we searched away from the dealers towards a footpath that bordered the dealership car pound and went into a park. If you put yourself into a criminal's mindset it was the perfect route for someone to make their exit. As we set off Sherlock was his usual bustling self. He always seems to be in a good mood even if we're on a late one. It doesn't seem to make any difference to him. We're together; he's happy. Sweet.

What I wasn't expecting was Sherlock to get a scent for something well before we got to the smouldering vehicles. His body language changed from just bobbing along to excited with a purposeful stride when we were still 600 metres away. In true retriever style he set off into the gloom – I couldn't see a thing; watching a black dog in complete darkness is quite a challenge – but when I broke out the flashlight I couldn't believe my eyes. He had indicated on a pair of latex gloves. It looked like the gloves had been discarded. Not only was the trace of accelerant going to be a valuable find for the CID team on site, but the gloves could have DNA on them, which could lead directly to someone they would undoubtedly want to question. This was credible evidence and once again it was Sherlock who was the specialist detective at the crime scene.

Sometimes when I watch Sherlock working as tightly and focused as that I think he resembles a clockwork toy, fully wound and moving without hesitation. He is a real work machine and I admire him for having his own sense of discipline. He was learning his trade fast and I was learning about him. Watching him, it's not difficult to see how far the dog and handler teams have come, and how the pioneering over the past twenty years has really made and continues to make a difference on the streets today, as the programme progresses and develops all the time. It's a real privilege to be part of this special band of brothers.

And then, Sherlock will look back at me, brown eyes wide, slobbering over his tennis ball reward, head cocked just so. Ahh, Sherlock, Rockster, Mr Bustle Britches and sometime 'Git!', you don't know how special you are.

Chapter 9

Fire: a Destructive Force

Fire strikes indiscriminately. It has no respect for age, gender, faith, wealth, health or status; it just takes down anything and anyone in its path. It hits and keeps hitting until it's extinguished. This means we have to approach every scene with an open mind, letting only the evidence tell the story. Worryingly, one of the increasingly common scenes that Sherlock and I are called out to are patches of scrubland, where people who have been displaced by politics, poverty, broken homes, splintered relationships and just having society turn a blind eye to them are forced to sleep rough in makeshift 'tented accommodation'. Very often these 'communities' include the most vulnerable individuals in our society – homeless youngsters, drug addicts, alcoholics and, ever more common now, women who have been given a tent and a sleeping bag on their release from prison. As you can imagine, it's a very sad and dangerous environment, where life itself is considered part of a currency of blankets, cigarettes, sex, drugs and alcohol.

One of the saddest days was when Sherlock and I were called out because a homeless man had been found burnt to death with his tent sealed around him. There were no witnesses to anything – which is not unusual. The tented community is very tight-knit in the presence of the authorities, and the locals are aware of people being there but take no more notice than that. A 'special post-mortem' had been requested by the police, which means that they wanted to know if the man was the victim of foul play, which most likely meant being beaten up for money, drugs or cigarettes and then set alight. Alternatively, death could have been by misadventure: getting drunk and then lighting a cigarette in the close confines of the tent and falling asleep ... that would just about do it.

The post-mortem revealed that there was no smoke in the airway, so the man was dead before the fire started – but was he killed and the fire lit by the murderer to cover their tracks? This was for Sherlock to help us figure out. If he were to detect the presence of an ignitable fluid then it would be likely it was used to try and destroy the evidence – in this case, the body.

I could see Sherlock's nose twitching and I appreciated that on a site like this where there are so many different scents to pick up his senses must have been really heightened. I decided to take him to one side for a chat: 'You all right, mate? It's not nice, this one, is it? Don't worry, none of us like these cases and I know it doesn't help when there's so much going on. Let's get away for a while and clear that nose of yours ...' I gave him a good old fuss and we did our usual and took ourselves off a good distance away from the area of origin of the fire and the charred grass.

That cold March morning we searched over two acres. We started well away from where the man's body was found and worked in towards that spot. We covered all the different routes that he could have taken to the site, so we could discount the presence of an ignitable liquid. We were also looking for anything that could have been used to set the fire – a rag or piece of clothing with liquid accelerant on it, which could have DNA on it too. But there was nothing to find and that's what we reported to the police on site. It was important to cover the whole site and surrounding area because everything and anything we found that turned out to be related to the deceased would have been a way of building a profile of how he died and his last moments, so that his family could have been informed and the case could progress. Although we couldn't yet know what had happened to the victim, the lack of the presence of an accelerant was just one element in the picture that the police would piece together.

Being so close to that kind of end-of-life experience so often makes you realise that there are some terrible ways to die. After two decades as a firefighter and now as an investigator I'm convinced that if fire was a person I wouldn't like them one bit. They would be the kind of selfish individual who simply *takes* from a situation, and if they give anything back at all it would be a negative energy – a person who would leave you feeling weak and depleted physically and emotionally. Fire would be a parasitical acquaintance you'd go to all lengths to avoid socially, just as a matter of self-protection. Sherlock would probably snarl at them and they wouldn't want to approach him and that would be enough for me (unless someone can give me a very good reason why I need to feel differently, I am, on the whole, suspicious of anyone who shies away from Sherlock).

Fires don't start on their own; they all have a source and sometimes the cause can be traced back to a human hand. I always think anyone who chooses fire as their weapon is revealing a lot about their own personality. Fire is silent, deadly, dramatic, destructive, violent, immediate, cowardly and cheap. It's the first choice for criminals who want to cover up or disguise another crime like murder or robbery by committing any incriminating evidence to the flames. People can start fires then walk away, never intending to face their victims. Anyone committing arson runs a tremendously high risk of being found guilty and handed a life sentence. It's a high price to pay but obviously there are people who are keen to take the risk.

What often makes fire so powerful is how we are still learning about its behaviour. Twenty Fenchurch Street (affectionately known as the Walkie Talkie) is an iconic building and instantly recognisable on the London skyline. But when it was first unveiled it caused interest on the ground as well as in the sky. Its glass-clad sides were acting like a giant magnifying glass, sparking radiated heat damage to parked cars three streets away. I'm guessing no one thought of that when they were putting the design together! But it's just one example of how fire performs and how it can catch us out because it's not always understood.

Most people think they know about fire because they've seen it in TV programmes and in films. Sometimes you hear people refer to fire as if they know it. As if it can be harnessed, predicted and controlled. They refer to it as a 'living thing'; they even talk of fire being beautiful, and about its 'dancing angels' in a way that's almost romantic. The big-screen American epics like *Backdraft* and *The Towering Inferno* portray fire as an uncontrollable monster and that's a more realistic way of looking at what is actually an unpredictable, relentless killer. From a firefighter's perspective we are careful to respect it, and as Fire Investigators we examine the science behind it.

When we talk about the Fire Triangle, it's usually to do with fire safety but the same applies if we're thinking about what makes fire 'happen'. It's a simple chemical reaction involving three elements – fuel, heat and oxygen – which all need to be present for a fire to ignite. So we understand that the three depend on each other to sustain the fire, and, consequently, if one is removed the fire would be prevented or extinguished. That's the classroom version, which is usually accompanied by the candle in a jar experiment: smother the oxygen and the fire can't survive. But what happens so often in house fires is that if the fuel supply is rich enough, the hot fire gases become smoke, and that smoke is then ignited by the fire. This is one of the dangers for firefighters trapped in spaces and why the hot gases in the smoke around them can, when they reach the right temperature, become the fire above them. Then fire is also a cold and merciless life-taker.

If you know the science behind fire, you'll know why so many instances of 'TV fire' are impossible: the lit cigarette dropped into the pool of petrol would not create a river of fire, for example. The cigarette would just go out! It's not the petrol that sets on fire, it's the vapour. That's why Sherlock is able to pick up the scent much easier in the residual warmth after a blaze, when the vapour from the accelerant is released and airborne.

The way we learn most of our lessons about the nature of fire is, sadly, through real-life incidents. The King's Cross fire, on 18 November 1987, claimed the lives of thirty-one people who were making their way through the station that evening including one firefighter, Soho's Station Officer Colin Townsley, who lost his life in the rescue mission. Never in its 124-year history had the London Underground suffered such a loss of life in a single incident, and how it happened intrigued Fire Investigators for years after the event because of the unique aspects of the fire dynamics. There were so many factors affecting the fire that day that it behaved 'differently'. Many years' worth of rubbish had collected under the wooden-slatted escalator, undisturbed, out of view; this, together with grease from the mechanism ignited by – possibly – a discarded cigarette, created a unique and unforeseen situation. The slow burn of the rubbish acted as the fuel and formed the basis of the killer blaze as all the necessary elements in the Fire Triangle – fuel, heat and oxygen – came together. It's believed that it created a flashover, as a sudden and rapid spread of heat caused by smoke or fumes igniting generated a massive explosion of fire overhead that raged and consumed all in its path.

As we learn from events such as the King's Cross fire, the information and elements of fire science helps us to progress the training for Fire Investigation Dogs. It's horrible that often an accident has to happen before we know the lesson is there to be learnt, but the opportunity to expand our knowledge means we are able to prevent more fires and save more lives in the future.

Chapter 10

Clever Sherlock!

I have gotten to know many of Sherlock's habits pretty well, but I'm not too pleased with his latest: I think Sherlock has taken up yodelling. It's either that or he's a budding werewolf. I remain undecided. One thing is for sure and that is that he has taken a sudden dislike to the electronic turn-out announcer and her annoying trumpets. No, that's not the name of a new band, it's the mobilising system that the London Fire Brigade introduced between 2001 and 2002 to replace the good old-fashioned alarm bells. We all used to respond to the bells going down but now we have a robotic voice telling us to 'mobilise! … mobilise!' and Sherlock loathes it.

Sherlock never knew the old bells, that was all before his time, and, to be fair, he didn't mind the funny air horn/trumpet arrangement of the new system to start with, but now it really grates on him. He's so funny to watch when the alarm goes off because his ears start to move up and down during the trumpet section, and then, when the woman's monotone voice kicks in, his lips go all wobbly, he throws his head back and HOWLS! He keeps going all the way through her announcements – that's every fifteen seconds up to ninety seconds (the crew aims to be gone in sixty seconds max) until she has finished. It's even worse when he's on shift and in the kennels. You can hear his serenade drift through the station – it's an eerie sound!

I guess that's the sound Sherlock associates with going out on a shout, or his friends leaving him to answer a fire call. For the men and women on Watch it's a call into the unknown that will result in them engaging in people's lives and maybe entering their homes too – and at the most challenging of times. Sherlock included. He is the master of the house search now. That's partly because he is so well practised, given that we carry out an average of three or four searches a week and deal with death all too regularly; and partly because he is, well, just the master.

'Come on, Sherlock, give the singing a break. This time the bells are going down for us too, mate. Time to get our kit on and hit the road. Where's your ball?'

It's very rare to see Sherlock without a ball or something in his mouth and I remember I was looking for a ball to take with us on the shout not realising that Sherlock was following me – with a ball in his mouth! 'Who's a clever dog then?' I said to him while he was probably wondering what on earth I was up to. 'Tell you what. You look after your toys and I'll look after my stuff. You like the sound of that?' He had known me long enough to ignore my sarcasm and plodded towards our dog van with just one backwards glance to let me know that he had heard me.

All I knew about this case was that fire had all but destroyed a large thatched cottage in north London and the owner had been taken to hospital with burn injuries. There was just something the attending Fire Investigator wasn't convinced about – something about the pattern of the fire that didn't fit. He knew that Sherlock would be able to rule some factors in or out and that's exactly what the investigation needed to establish further lines of inquiry.

The cottage was a shell and would most likely have to be pulled down at the end of the investigation. The thatched roof had created a particular fire dynamic – as if someone had put a haystack on top of the burning house. Thankfully the house had been empty – we learned that it had been up for sale for a long time – and local witnesses reported that the first they heard of any trouble that night was a noise: a 'boom'! This would have been created by the over-pressure in the closed-off house. Conflicting reports of a 'fire ball' in the hallway and 'two shadowy figures' also in the hallway made Sherlock's presence all the more vital.

There was so much damage and debris on the floor that we were certain Sherlock would be searching what was left of this property twice over: that's before and after the excavation. Doing my risk assessment for Sherlock I could see there were plenty of areas that my dog detective would find very interesting – it was possible he would find something that would help the police narrow down their options. I went to collect Sherlock from the van which was parked a distance from the search area.

He was raring to go. He only needs to take one look at me dressed in my familiar marshmallow outfit and he knows we're going to work. Tail wagging and ears twitching up and down as if they were on a seesaw, I knew he was ready. We were going to walk into this scene and see if there was anything of interest en route. There was nothing until we reached the car parked outside the house. Sherlock was all over it …

It was like he was fitted with Duracell batteries! Indications started to roll in; first on a rag in the boot, but strangely not on the nozzle that you would need for a fuel can – that looked unused. My first thought was maybe the CCTV at the local garage would have picked up someone collecting the fuel in cans. That was something I suggested to police on the team.

Bustling and sniffing, Sherlock's keen nose led him to the front entrance. Now *this* was a Fire Dog on full speed, as he got the smell of something potentially incriminating under his nose. He was standing on top of the thatch that had fallen from the roof which had hung over the porch. There was a large amount of debris on the floor, reaching up to a height of between one to two metres, and Sherlock was very excited about it. His paws were dancing and tapping and his head and eyes were shifting from side to side: 'Over here, Dad! I found something ... Look at me! Dad ... over here!' It was a positive indication that the police SOCO was waiting for. Sherlock was pulling hard at his lead and it took all of my energy to hold him back from diving nose-first into the remnants of the roof.

'Just to say, I think what you might be looking for is under that lot,' I advised the police, and then drew Sherlock away to give him some praise for a job well done. I let him go through to the hall and kitchen and I stood on the threshold between the two and gave my dog a lot of fuss – and I mean a *lot* of fuss. Not the ball, though. It wasn't time for the ball. He still had work to do.

Sherlock completed a full and thorough house search in less than fifteen minutes and indicated an incredible nine times. 'You just do the job, Sherlock … and this time you smashed it, mate!'

The following day Mick Boyle was next on shift and took Murphy and Roscoe in to conduct the post-excavation search. Searching a second time after the fire debris has been removed is always a good idea because the heat that's retained in the building can release the vapour from an ignitable liquid or solid, and that's going to hit a dog's sensitive nose like a freight train. As Sherlock had done the previous day, the dogs were able to get under the floorboards – and pop out again (thank goodness) – indicating areas of interest; they moved on through with their heads going up and down to catch the vapours, and then darting around again to pin the scent to the point where it was at its strongest. Roscoe and Murphy raced over to the window where Sherlock had indicated so positively on the thatch with me the day before, and the excavation had revealed why: unbeknownst to us several petrol cans had been lurking under the thatch. Clever, Sherlock!

As an investigator I go in to a scene with an open mind, looking for evidence that points to or from arson. The devil isn't always in the detail, hiding under great big piles of thatch. Sometimes he's staring you in the face, because even the most dedicated arsonist can occasionally let themselves down. This was what happened with one case, which I will always remember as 'the one with the wheelie bins'.

Not too long after the thatched cottage case, we were called out one morning to a house in High Wycombe. It was a huge detached house, backing on to superb open – and highly accessible – countryside, which always makes me twitch with suspicion. We understood the owner had been trying to sell for some time. Apparently, lots of work had been done but it fell short of the building standards regulations. The fire was out when we arrived, which was possibly because the ignitable vapours had gone past their upper explosive limit (UEL). All ignitable liquids 'light' at different concentrations in the air, so they can light and then, when they reach their UEL, they'll go out again. With this in mind the fire pattern made us think there could be multiple areas of origin.

Thankfully no one was in the house at the time of the fire, which is always a relief to know, and especially when we saw the state of this house. It wasn't a pretty sight, for sure. I was particularly keen for Sherlock to search a huge area. I figured it would be good experience, and I wagered he would enjoy the hunt outside in the overgrown field, although I hoped he wouldn't spot any wildlife: he was there to do a job, which meant no distractions. Based on previous encounters I'd say he was more of a people 'person' than an animal 'person', but come to think of it, he did chase a badger once in training. Probably because he thought it was a whole lot of fun, not realising that the badger's cat-like hissing was telling Sherlock to 'Get lost, pal!' He may not be too bothered by badgers but he particularly dislikes foxes – they really don't get along – so I was hoping we could give them a miss on this job.

With no sign of any distracting wildlife, it didn't take long to get Sherlock focused on the task at hand. From the moment we started to search outside the back and side of the property he was interested. But it was when we reached the front that his eyes started to roll, and that slow deliberate pace told me that he was on to something – he just needed to fix on it. I watched him closely. He was homing in on the row of wheelie bins, and one in particular. He was doing a lot of pirouetting and trying to reach up the side of one of them. I could tell that he wanted to look inside!

There was only one thing to do – I lifted him up and let him have a sniff inside. It was full. Now I had a really excited dog on my hands. This is the moment, as a dog handler, when a mini alarm bell goes off in your head: has he detected an accelerant, or has he sniffed out someone's cooked chicken carcass and reckons he's found his second breakfast? But there was something about Sherlock's demeanour that told me he was serious about this bin. Really serious. In he went – like a demented mole! I had to drag him out of it because whatever he was after was clearly right at the bottom. I pulled the bin bags out for him and there it was right at the bottom – a bottle of BBQ lighter fluid in a sealed bag. Thank you, Sherlock. And it wasn't just me saying that, it was all of the Thames Valley Police present. The local fire service had only recently had to give up their Fire Investigation Dog Team due to budget cuts and here we were, reminding them of their worth.

In all, Sherlock highlighted nine areas of interest in the property, alongside the lighter fluid, and we managed to pin down the peculiar fire pattern that had raised suspicions in the first place – all the doors and uPVC windows had been closed during the blaze, meaning the fire had been deprived of oxygen. And what was extra-special about the results of our work was that the lighter fluid bottle had a child-lock on the cap, which was most likely smothered in DNA. The SOCO looked pretty pleased with that find and was pretty pleased with Sherlock too.

As I was congratulating Sherlock on his tremendous work I heard one of the team say: 'Did you say you were looking for the Fire Dog Handler? Oh, he's over there rolling on the floor … with his dog.' That's called celebrating!

In his civvies, Sherlock is the girls' 'naughty friend' – that's what they call him. But in uniform he is the Fire Investigation Dog for the London Fire Brigade, an operative at the cutting edge of fire science, helping to put criminals behind bars. And as my great friend Clive says, there's no perfect crime – especially if you have a dog on the team. I agree, and after five years doing this job with Sherlock I know that an investigation begins when the Fire Investigation Dog arrives, and it finishes when we are finished. If we're on site, then our search will be thorough, and for Sherlock that may only mean five to ten minutes of focused work to bring indisputable results. If we have to use the Gastec in Sherlock's absence, it would take us in excess of six to eight hours to cover the same area, and the technology still doesn't register down to the levels that a dog's nose does. A human nose has about 2 million scent receptors, compared to a dog's which has 200 million receptors, which is why Sherlock's nose is so good and accurate for the work that we do – and why he is always there in a flash the moment food appears!

Believe me, when we've completed our search and he is off duty he is happy to be the focus of attention – and he's never short of that. Everyone loves Sherlock. Particularly on the most challenging of cases, it's not unusual to see the teams kneel down to give Sherlock some fuss and offer thanks for his help and, I think, for just being there.

I'm very fortunate because I get a great deal of job satisfaction knowing that we are helping to solve crime and piece people's lives back together, but also our work is vital in building our knowledge of the unpredictable force of fire, potentially saving lives in the future. Sometimes the days are tough, but knowing I have someone right beside me, to share the darkness in the aftermath of a fatality, and the high tension of a positive indication that could contribute to a guilty individual getting their just desserts, is a welcome comfort. And not just share that darkness, but brighten it. I'm not alone in this job and I'm thankful for that.

Chapter 11

When All Hope is Lost

As much as Sherlock would like to think he's the brains of our outfit, working with Sherlock means that to a certain extent I have to think for both of us. There's an element of second-guessing in our work, in that I'm taking in what he is doing and what he is finding and merging it with my own observations. And rather than that being a downside, I find that it can be a real positive. Therefore, as Sherlock's handler, I need to be thinking ahead – in fact, rather like when playing snooker, it's always about thinking at least three moves ahead. For example, when attending a case where we already know there is a fatality, we need to be aware that there could be at least one more. I need to be sure that Sherlock is safe, that I am preparing him well for the search by talking to him quietly and showing him the ball to work for, and making sure that I watch his body language to help him and read him as he works ahead of me; and at the same time I have to be anticipating what might lie just around the corner.

What I can't prepare Sherlock for are the quirks of human nature. I can't do that because I sometimes don't understand them myself. I often find myself thinking – to pinch a phrase used by my colleagues in the North – that there really is 'nowt so queer as folk'. In my training I had to study human behaviour, and one case study was an incident of a burned-out car that the first responders from the fire service had to attend. The man who dialled 999 was the same person who, when the fire engine arrived, threw himself into his burning car. That still horrifies me and probably always will. As will the sight of the man stuck to his bath after soaking himself in white spirit and setting himself alight. I could never forget the expression on his partner's face when she opened the bathroom door to see the horror. Neither of these two victims left a note. No explanation of their actions. I guess sometimes there are no words and no reason why. Things just are.

Fire is a link in all these cases, and Sherlock and my presence is very often at the end of the line. How these people reached that point is often unclear and undocumented. All we can do is try to piece together their last moments on earth, so the police can make sense of it and give their loved ones some kind of closure. Mental health is a huge concern for all of us. One in four people will suffer some form of mental health issue in our lifetime, so instead of it being the proverbial elephant in the room, it is something we are all being encouraged to talk about and seek help for. For those of us in the Emergency Services, dealing with mental health issues is not new. It is something we meet, in some capacity, every working day.

One time when we were called to a house fire and fatality, we were told that it was almost certain that it was a case of a mother being killed by her son. Even just a little background on the family helps to knit together the how and why of a case, and it certainly assisted here. It transpired that the mother had had concerns about her son's mental health for some time, and she had shared those concerns with her local mental health team. In the twenty-four hours leading up to the fire she had been in touch with the team and the police to say that she feared for her life and wanted her son sectioned for his protection as well as her own. A mother knows her children and this mother was right to be afraid.

This was a sad case from the start and there was nothing we could do for that mother except trace those final moments and contribute to the evidence that would, hopefully, result in the son gaining the help he needed. This was a criminal investigation and Sherlock and I worked with the police, helping them to put the facts and the evidence in place. It was a big search of a large Victorian property and grounds, and as is our normal practice, we walked in from a distance before stepping through the blue-and-white tape at 200 metres from the house. We started by searching the street: approximately 200 metres by 20 metres including front garden. We didn't know at this point if anything had been left in the street or front garden – if it had Sherlock would find it.

It was a hot day, and I was certainly feeling it, but Sherlock was happy with the search to the house and was totally unbothered by the heat. Good job he was wearing his summer coat and we had plenty of water, because this was already shaping up to be a long day. Settling into his 'business as usual' stride, Sherlock skipped along until he reached the property. It was as if he took one whiff of the place and went literally into a spin. I was going into the search with a whirling dervish: his senses must have been buzzing, but I had seen this before and I knew that he would calm. I got him to sit, and I showed him the ball – his prize – whispered the trigger words, and with a soft tap on head he was off. He started searching the first room from one side to the other, left then right, quartering the ground in good gun-dog fashion. He was responsive and positive and knew exactly what I wanted him to do – without me asking.

We moved from room to room, opening and closing the doors as we went, Sherlock with his nose to the ground, even sniffing under the door as we went through. I wanted to make sure that he didn't get carried away and miss something, but I needn't have worried, he was absolutely on top of it.

In the living room Sherlock indicated on a bookcase and the base of a stool; in a bedroom he indicated on the base of the bed. All this pointed to the fire having multiple areas of origin. What was odd about this case, however, was the presence of numerous BBQ lighter blocks at each of Sherlock's indication points, all piled on top of each other, clearly meant to get the fire going – but they hadn't taken. If they had all burnt away, the accelerant would still have been traceable, but having the scent of the 'neat' product hidden there was really exciting for Sherlock, and he was happy to take all the praise for his hard work. Everyone was delighted to see a dog on the case and, as had happened before, one of the police officers asked me: 'Do you mind if I stroke your dog and take a photo of him?' Of course I didn't mind. I was thrilled! Sherlock had done a thorough search and a great job.

It had taken Sherlock merely twenty minutes to complete the search of both inside and outside the property. And yet the evidence we gathered could prove to be vital when the officers from the borough CID and Murder Incident Team (MIT) continued the investigation. For the time being, our part was over.

Sherlock and I are all too aware of the responsibility that comes with our job and we take our roles very seriously. None more so than in the case of arson. According to the Arson Prevention Forum, arson costs the British economy billions of pounds a year, with just under 50 per cent of all reported fires in England considered deliberate. And yet this powerful force of heat and flame is something we still don't fully understand. Without Fire Investigation Dogs like Sherlock, as with Star, Odin, Sam, Roscoe and Murphy before him, so many more cases would go unsolved, letting the guilty go free, while the victims' families remain heart-broken and without justice.

The best way to catch an arsonist is to think like an arsonist. What would they use? Where would they throw the can or the gloves or the rag afterwards? Think about the placing of the petrol, or lighter fluid – whatever their choice of weapon – and imagine what they were trying to achieve. Stepping beyond the tape as a Fire Investigator and imagining all of these things doesn't feel odd because it's just another tool in the box. After all, it's the same as what a police officer says you need to do to catch a thief.

One such case was of a rugby clubhouse valued at in excess of £1 million in Surrey had gone up in smoke and the owner was understandably mad keen on finding out who did it. The fire was still burning when the Fire Investigator arrived on the scene, which gave him the opportunity to follow the burn pattern of the fire. Burn patterns are laden with clues as to how a fire progressed, but also how it started. There was something odd about the pattern so my colleague from Surrey Fire and Rescue Service felt that it was time to call on Sherlock's skills.

When we arrived, the area wasn't safe for Sherlock to search right away, so it gave me a chance to take a look around and borrow Sherlock's detective deerstalker attitude. I walked the grounds and the local area, the footpaths and car parks. So many places where, if accelerants had been used, they could have been discarded. I put myself in the position of the arsonist and worked out Sherlock's search area – which was huge, a perimeter of some 1,000 metres, not including the work to quarter the ground and track through footpaths. But I knew that he could do it because he always wants to search. All we had to do was wait until the firefighting had been completed and there was no risk of heat underfoot, so he could go in and do his stuff. He would then search again following the excavation of the scene to identify if there were any additional areas where his target substances had been trapped in by the debris.

After the perimeter search, it was on with the boots for this one; with broken tiles and brick damage underfoot I couldn't risk Sherlock cutting a pad or getting a twist of metal or a nail in his paw. He didn't put up much of a fight, just the usual case of rigid legs until the boots were on. Sherlock loves the outdoors so the exterior searches are, I think, his favourite, and this one certainly grabbed his interest. When he reached a low wall at the rear of the building he began to show interest in the timber part of the structure. I knew from Sherlock's body language that there was an accelerant on it and the forensic team's laboratory analysis later confirmed that it was BBQ lighter gel, an uncommon form of ignitable substance. Combining this information with the V-shaped burn pattern at the rear of the building was all the police needed as evidence. Following excavation, Sherlock identified a further area where some of the gel had been dropped on the floor, which had been covered by fire debris. Sherlock was the hero of the day. He was the hero all over again when the same gel was found to have been used in a number of other arson attacks across the county, managing to link the seemingly unrelated incidents all to one suspect! It was Sherlock's nose, not my detective thinking, that was the reason for nailing this important piece of evidence in a case that was baffling the police and causing – although no deaths – a great deal of criminal damage to wooden pavilions and club houses throughout Surrey.

In our day-to-day job, Sherlock and I deal with the how not the why when it comes to investigating fires, but I often wonder if Sherlock has a good old chuckle at some human beings and their antics. If he does, I wonder what he would have thought of the day when I was a young firefighter on a call out to a house where the back rooms had been blown clean off the side of the building. The person living there had been producing 'honey oil' by extracting sap from cannabis using butane gas. Using an explosive gas in the close confines of a living room in a shared house was never going to be a good idea. A lesson this person found out the hard way. It still amazes me the lengths people will go to where drugs are concerned. One way or another, drugs are bad and will harm and could even kill you – if not today then most likely tomorrow.

However, with scenes like this we musn't let the funny side of things drop our guard. We have to remain vigilant to what may be around us. In that scene, we could have still been surrounded by danger if there was still something in there that hadn't yet exploded. Recent world events have made a fear of terrorist attacks a firm fixture in our psyche and in this job we have a heightened awareness of what could happen to others if we miss something. There is also the awareness of the potential of being a target ourselves, which was the case for some firefighters attending a blaze at a home in the outskirts of London. The team were bravely tackling the flames, only to find that the arsonists had set what appeared to be an Improvised Explosive Device (IED) as a criminal booby-trap in the microwave and set it to detonate after the crew had arrived. They used a timer, as you would for turning your lights on when you're on holiday. So cold and calculating, but fortunately foiled: on arrival the crew had disconnected the mains services to the property so the timer failed. Sherlock was on form that day too. He searched the house thoroughly and came across two different sections of interest. He found liquid on the laminate flooring and on the stair carpet. It had been sloshed about and not destroyed by the fire, so it was easy for Sherlock to find. His nose will score accurately on anything up to a year old once the ignitable fluid is no longer present but is merely an essence left behind. There really is nothing better than a dog's nose for the job.

Although working with fire is a dangerous job, Sherlock doesn't see the danger; he sees getting out of the station as a chance to run about and get a lot of fuss from many generous souls. But once in a while there's a chance to have a giggle, and Sherlock is always up for that. I think dogs have a sense of humour and we don't often give them credit for their ability to make us laugh. There was one occasion when we had been called to search a flat. Sherlock probably thought the man sitting on the sofa in the flat was up for a chat. He was sitting quietly even though he was already in handcuffs and asked, strangely, if he could watch Sherlock work. Normally we try to keep the scene as sterile as possible so that it can't be contaminated, but I didn't know that the police still had the suspect in the property when Sherlock and I went in. Taking one sniff, Sherlock headed through the living room and into the kitchen, where he indicated on a carrier bag in a kitchen cupboard. The suspect had said that there weren't any ignitable liquids in the property prior to the search, but lo and behold, the carrier bag contained a massive bottle of white spirit! 'That's not looking good, mate!' was the understatement from the police officer. It's at moments like this that Sherlock shows that time and time again, he really is top dog: he doesn't need me at all sometimes, but I always need him.

Chapter 12

A Very Good Boy

What makes Sherlock so good at his job is his energy and drive. Most dogs are born with natural skills that can be honed and trained. We are teaching the dogs a job that we can't do ourselves – we just don't have the nose for it – and the great thing about the job is that the dogs love sniffing. It comes naturally to them. When I'm with Sherlock, putting him through his paces I'm still in awe of him. I see him eye up a new challenge and then I recognise that 'I'm working this out' look, which is accompanied by lots of stomping and ear-wagging, and then he slows almost to a standstill before spinning off again, constantly on the hunt for the next scent.

That's the thing with Sherlock, he just doesn't stop searching for new adventures. Sometimes he looks for them in his sleep. His eyes will be closed – well, just about – and he does this snake-eyes side look, where he looks like he's watching what you're up to but he's actually asleep. And there's always at least one toe that will be twitching – he is never perfectly still. I admire his stamina. When he falls asleep in the garden or in the house, he always looks as if he's getting ready to chase something – as if every muscle in his body is tense and taut, ready to leap into action. I imagine him dreaming of running though the dewy grass with his sporty ancestors, all of them looking athletic and handsome and then sometimes a little bit daft too – just like him. And when he's not running in his dreams he's throwing shapes with his legs in the air and his long ears flopped down on the ground. And when he really gets into snoring, his lips fall back over his teeth and they wobble as he breathes. He looks so happy. At least I know what he's up to if he's lying in his spot in the kitchen or at my feet in the office. As long as he's not slobbering on my shoes.

This bundle of fun, determination, affection and down-right loveliness is my dog and I'm proud of that. I see him look to me when we are out on a search and, though I'm sure he's not aware of it, I look to him too. We're a team facing a challenge with every shout we attend. When the bells go down it's not just me that has to be ready to go, it's Sherlock too – and he never fails to jump to it and see what the day brings in the way of walks, food, excitement, fuss and people. Apart from his hatred of traffic, I never see fear in Sherlock and I hope I never will. Being a Fire Dog is a responsible job and we know he loves it because he's always smiling, even if it is with a ball in his mouth! Even after a long day at work he will still have energy to spare when we go to the park at the back of our house. He runs off as soon as we get there to find something to do involving mud. I can stop to talk to people or they will come over to me and chat about Sherlock and he's always there in the background. If he comes closer I just know the person I'm talking to will get a mud shower. He doesn't spare the horses when he's on a dig – it's Australia or bust! That's his style and it has been from when he was a puppy.

Sometimes concerns are raised for the welfare of dogs who are trained to assist human beings, maybe through military service or helping someone suffering a disability, or, like Sherlock, having a job in public service. Members of the public want reassurance that the dogs are happy in their work and are being well cared for and provided with everything they should be: a suitable place to live, a proper diet, the freedom to show normal behaviour patterns, to be kept with or apart from other animals (if that's appropriate), and to be protected from pain, injury, suffering and disease.

Sherlock lives with our family, so he can tick off the welfare needs in very quick succession. Like other dogs he likes to please his humans, and because all his training is based on play and reward Sherlock and his mates are not just learning new skills, they are having a great time too!

Despite all of this, in the early days of the Fire Dog project in 1996, some concerns relating to the long-term welfare of the dogs were raised. Clive Gregory was happy to address these on behalf of the West Midlands Fire Service, where the project was first launched. He approached a local veterinary surgery to help with dogs deployed to cold fire scenes who were tasked with searching for accelerant residues in burnt fire debris. Clive was convinced that there would not be a problem, considering that his own dog Star, the original Fire Dog, had been looked after by the same surgery. Throughout Star's life they had monitored him and looked at any possible damage to his health as a result of exposure to fire-debris residues.

Medical checks on Star included X-rays, blood and urine tests and heart monitoring, and no adverse effects of fire-scene exposure were found. Star enjoyed a full life, retired as a family pet, and died in 2007, just shy of his thirteenth birthday. He carried out this work for most of his life, but due to the limited exposure of the dog's respiratory system to the fire debris no damage to health was incurred. The dogs are carrying out a reasonable number of searches – being operational for an average of three or four days in a week – working to a rapid timescale to complete their tasks quickly and, at the same time, extremely efficiently. And as such they are not being exposed to anything harmful to their health.

As I said, Sherlock relies on me for his welfare needs – that's everything from his bed for the night, his grub and his healthcare. As for being able to 'exhibit normal behaviour' I think the craters in the local park and the areas of my garden which now resemble a section of the battlefield on the Somme are testimony to the fact that Sherlock gets a fair chance to express himself as a dog! When he travels, it's in a climate-controlled dog van, and when he is on duty he has a specially padded harness, a selection of leads of differing lengths, and boots to protect his feet from sharp objects on the ground. Although the dogs enter fire scenes to search they are *never* sent into hot scenes. The boots are to protect from broken glass and splinters and crumbled masonry, not heat. No risks are ever taken with our dogs and that is why there has never been an injury to a Fire Dog while they have been on duty. Sherlock has his uniform as I have mine, but we never forget that we are working with a dog who needs love and care as well as health and safety protection.

But no matter how long you're a firefighter or a Fire Dog, fire never stops being scary. It is something we should respect, but being afraid of it is probably one of the reasons why we hold back on learning more about it. Everything about fire is scientific and as investigators we use science to understand why fire has occurred in a particular place, and its behaviour gives us clues as to whether something has been present to make it behave differently, and if so what it was. Sherlock is invaluable in that process, invaluable as a tool for accuracy. That's the beauty of science: it's not woolly and vague. In a similar way, dogs are honest and packed with integrity, so it's a good match.

Although we are still learning more about fire, human behaviour around fire is far more predictable. For instance, if we go to a hotel, an exhibition or a concert we will have it in our heads that if we need to get out then we will go to where we came in. But think about it. If everyone tries to get out the way they came in all at the same time, actually very few people will make it outside. There will be a crush and many will die. It's a sad fact that when people don't make it, often their bodies will be found by the door – the door they came in by. If they had used other exits there wouldn't have been a crush and they just might have made it. Some will try to hide behind the door instinctively; wherever they are, children will go to a dark, safe place like a wardrobe or cupboard or under the bed. And when it's all over, that's where they are found, huddled up against the flames, or, more likely, beaten by the smoke.

You can't make friends with fire and it can't always be controlled, so it's wise to think ahead and know what you are going to do when faced with one. If you find yourself in a large venue or any hotel just familiarise yourself with the exits, and visit the one that's closest to your room, so you know where it is. Do that whenever you go to the restaurant or the pool, just have the exits in your head. Go up and touch the door. That way it will stay in your mind without becoming something to panic about, should you need to use it. And be observant when you're out. We all run a semi-conscious mini profile on people we meet on trains, on buses and in coffee shops; we're doing it all the time, without really thinking. Being more observant is a good thing and so is going with your gut instinct – and reporting anything you find suspicious. This isn't scary – it's about staying safe.

Spending time with Sherlock at work and at play is a great way for me to banish all those grim thoughts that this job can stir up. I'm lucky that he's at my side and

I have him to talk to about all kinds of things. And he makes me laugh with his idiosyncrasies. More and more of his cheeky side is developing and seeping into work-mode Sherlock as he makes the job his own. Hopefully it won't be long before he will be able to teach a new canine recruit some of his funny little ways that we have all come to know and love. One of my favourites in the Sherlock repertoire is 'Ash Angels'. This is when he lies down at a fire scene and swishes his tail from side to side, like someone making a snow angel, and creates a V-shape with his bottom in the dust!

Just as I need my downtime to process the events of the day, there's no doubt about it, Sherlock enjoys his 'me time' in the garden after work. Usually he will look around for something to chew, bite or just carry in his mouth. He's a bit like an only child looking for ways to entertain himself and he always finds something to hold his attention. If it's a ball, then he will lie with it in between his paws and after a session of licking and biting to soften the fuzzy covering he will start to peel it all off, bit by bit, until he's left with the shiny shell underneath. Now this is when he gets inventive, and I really admire him: he holds the ball really tightly and then … it pops up out from between his paws and he dashes after it! Sometimes he runs around with it in his own game of tennis-ball football, and then tries to catch it out by pouncing on it. He can keep this up for ages. To Sherlock it's 'see a ball and have some fun', and he never misses a chance for that. I've not timed him, but I'd say it takes him less than an hour to strip a ball down to bare rubber, and after that it depends whether he has it on his list for total destruction in one sitting, or if he has something else lined up and has plans to return to it later. I'm always fascinated by his choice because it never seems random. They either join the line-up of bald, chewed-up balls or they disappear. It always seems as if he has a bigger plan somehow; as if he is really thinking about how and when his toys should meet their doom. Perhaps that's just how Sherlock unwinds and lets the day run off him.

Although he is never far from a tennis ball, he likes other toys too. Right now, he is working through his Christmas collection, which comprises of a soft-toy snowman and a collection of rubber plum puddings with squeakers. The snowman is a bit grey but he's still got his little hat, scarf and carrot nose. So he's surviving well and will probably live through a few washes. I usually buy Sherlock's toys because I need to make sure they are the tough, spaniel-proof variety: this boy can really see them off if they are not up to the job. But to be without a tennis ball is like being up a creek without a paddle – not a great place to be, especially as one of these green fuzzy jobs is also Sherlock's reward at work. The Rockster here gets through fifty to sixty of the things every year. I always make sure there's a supply in the van, in the works car, in the house, in his kennel, at the station and on my person. It's not unusual for me to be caught out when I go for my wallet in a shop; usually I have to juggle with a ragged, soggy tennis ball before I can reach anything in my pocket.

Sherlock is fond of a comfort blanket. He likes to always have something in his mouth to carry around with him and chew on. If he was a baby he would be addicted to his dummy; if he was a pipe smoker, like his detective namesake, he would have that pipe in his mouth from dawn to dusk, whether it had tobacco in it or not. He just loves to chew! The consequences of that, for me, are … squelchy. Just as new parents are forever wandering around with dribbles of baby-sick on their shoulder, I have a similar experience with Sherlock and the slime he wipes on my trousers. Sometimes it's not the innocent tennis ball that's to blame. Sometimes it's his old favourite – the soggy sock. Sherlock is a sock thief. He doesn't need any encouragement when it comes to getting his paws on a sock. I once made the mistake of mislaying a white sports sock – only for Sherlock to find it. I saw him trailing it around the garden and, once I realised what it was, I made a dive for it before he bolted it down. He does that. As you zone in on him he tries to eat it quicker! He had this one tight between his teeth. Down went his shoulders, bottom in the air and back legs rooted to the floor, feet apart. He wasn't going to let go. What had I got myself into here? So began the tug o' war: first my way, then his way, my way, his way … I hoped no one was watching us. My way, his way … my way … his way, his way, his way … with half a ripped sock! 'Sherlock! Come back, you daft, daft dog!'

I don't recommend chasing a very fit spaniel around your garden unless you're prepared for the long game. There he was, having a great time, ears flapping and tail whipping everything it crashed into. There was only one way out of this for me: that was to get that sock away from him before it did a disappearing act – down his throat. I spied a stray tennis ball and approached him to do a trade: 'Come on, Sherlock, you know you like the ball better … You know you do … Hand over the sock, you awkward whatsit!' Clearly, he wanted both in his mouth at the same time, but I was on to him! As he stuck his jaw out for the ball his lips slackened enough for me to go for the sock. Phew! 'Well, my dear Sherlock, I would call that a victory – for me!' Or would I … ?

It's good to feel so pleased with yourself over such a small victory, but Sherlock was about to teach me a lesson. What had I done with the other section of ripped-apart sock? Yes, that's right, I had left it in the garden. Had Sherlock forgotten about it? Of course not. By the time I did the calculation in my head it was too late: the piece of sock was nowhere to be seen and that could only mean one thing. At least there was one saving grace – it wasn't a full sock. That could have caused the blockage of the century. The vet confirmed my first thought – we'd have to wait and sit it out. As I had already travelled this way before, I knew that it could be a very long wait …

After two and a half weeks I was on the verge of going back to the vet with my concerns and my sock-eating dog when I had a ghastly experience in his kennel. I could smell something really vile. And I mean repulsive. I tracked it down to where the stench was getting unbearable and put out my hand to what looked like a sausage. It wasn't a sausage. It had never been a sausage. But maybe, maybe … it had been part of a white sock. It was grassy, brown and very, very stinky. While we were waiting in sock hell, Sherlock had, at some point, sicked up the sock and secreted it amongst his treasures!

Irrespective of whether he's on duty or off, Sherlock is a bundle of energy and fun: that's Sherlock to a T. Fire can be a terrifying force, especially as we continue to learn more and more about its behaviour, but with all these questions that remain to be answered, at least we can always count on Sherlock to be his cheeky self!

Chapter 13

Just Another Day

'There's a part of me that hopes there is a God who watches over us on earth and that there's another place we go when we die. But there are times when I struggle with that and wonder, with so much hatred and violence in the world, would anyone's god really allow so much suffering?'

Yes, that's me ... I said that. It's the firefighter talking. The firefighter that's been inside me for half my life. Sometimes he comforts me and reassures me that everything that has passed is where it should be – in the past. Sometimes he niggles at me and makes me question myself, the universe and why every working day we see so many examples of man's inhumanity to man. As I've been thinking such things for a long time now, I'm guessing it goes with the job.

Six thirty a.m. and the Thames looks really beautiful. Calm. Sherlock is paddling on the foreshore in the slack water and I can see he's tempted to take a dip. He keeps looking across to me as if I'm going to make his mind up for him but he's on his own with that one. It's sunny but it's cold for a September morning and I wish I had grabbed my fleece before leaving Dowgate. I try to bring Sherlock down here whenever I can because I think he loves this time of day and this place as much as I do. For me, it's quality thinking time – no one around, being at one with nature, and the city still half asleep.

I'm looking at him now, standing in the shallow water, the yellow sun on his face and the silver reflection of the water creating a bit of a halo around his head.

There are times when I'm over-thinking things, about the report I've just read and the images I've just seen of a family lost in the flames of a house we are about to search, and then I glance over at Sherlock. He'll be smiling because he's at work and every outing for him is a chance to meet new people and run off some of his boundless energy. It's comforting to have him there, and reassuring because he doesn't change. He is the constant. To all of us in the London Fire Brigade Investigation Team Sherlock is one of us: he is a skilled investigator, he wears a uniform, and he reacts when the bells go down. He'd probably go to the gym, go for a pint and then enter a doughnut-eating competition if I let him.

When the Fire Brigade is called out they land as a team, as a single unit, more like a battalion of ground-force troops than one of the Emergency Services. As a body of men and women they are ready to tackle the enemy, which, in our case, is fire. Each individual on a Watch will have a specific role to play. Everything about you has to be focused on the job. The job comes first, or someone's life is at risk. Weak links are a danger to themselves and to everyone around them. A Watch Manager will drill their crew over and over to get the timing of each element of the firefighting procedure down to perfection. That's because a slick routine produces an efficient crew, so when the chips are down the team can go in together and look out for each other. If they don't, then someone could die.

Your priority? To search and rescue casualties before you become one yourself. Your judgement must be crystal clear – even if you feel that dreaded prickly sensation as your ears and face start to burn, and you know your hair will sizzle as the smoke around you threatens to become the fire above you. You have to carry on and you have to get it right. You're a firefighter and it's your job to save lives. Always second-guessing, and clicking into automatic pilot to do exactly what needs to be done to safeguard others. It's a way of being and that discipline never leaves you.

Before Sherlock, I had always been a little bit of a loner at work, as often happens when you are a Fire Investigator. It's not that you want to be; it's just the nature of your job: going out to the fire but not fighting the fire; searching the building for clues and causes but working with individuals from other agencies ... It's different. Even as a firefighter I was always intrigued about the back story of every case and wanted to know more about what had happened to bring about the dreadful circumstances. I wanted to follow the story and the investigator's job satisfied a lot of those questions for me. But then, when I got Sherlock, it was more like being part of a team again.

If I had seen Sherlock's CV before he took the job with me I imagine it would have listed skills and interests something like this ...

- Hole digger
- Tennis-ball modifier
- Sock eater (ex-chewer of shoes)
- Soft toy expert
- Yodelling student – sometimes several times a day
- Fire Investigation Dog – destined for greatness

Destined for greatness indeed. It's not really difficult to see why we signed him up to our team. Sherlock's potential and intelligence had been clear enough for Clive to fast-track him through his training from the age of five months. People expected great things of him then and he didn't disappoint anyone, least of all me.

Seven thirty a.m. beside the Thames and the sun is warmer but not warm enough to stay out any longer. While I've been pondering things Sherlock decided to go from paddling to a quick dip in the silvery water and take advantage of the shallow swell. I don't blame him as it is such a beautiful morning, a great way for both of us to ease ourselves into the uncertainty of our working day.

'That's enough now, mate. Time to go and do some work ...' Sherlock slowly stomps out of the water and I look round for the towel to dry him off. Oh no ... he's caught up with me, no towel ... and here comes the big spaniel shake-and-go! 'Sherlock! You ... !'

Chapter 14

Dreams can Come True

I was having such an exciting time with Sherlock, and work-wise everything was dropping into place for me. Saying that, it was, and still is, a lot of hard work but that isn't a problem because I am living my dream. And it really was a dream. And the journey here hasn't been easy by any means …

I suppose I always knew that I would end up in some kind of uniform, and that was my granddad's influence. I used to listen to him talking about serving with Field Marshal Montgomery and his Desert Rats in the Second World War, hours of stories and not a second of it wasted on me because I soaked it up, every word. My maternal grandparents were an inspirational lot too, and on that side of the family I had the pull of the RAF from my grandpa.

I was never short of hearing a tale or two of either of their adventures. My dad was inspirational in a different way – he had been a stockbroker for the majority of his life and loathed it. So, to stop me heading anywhere near that slippery slope, he took me into his office and showed me why he hated his career. Before the stock market, he had worked in television on wildlife programmes, which was his passion, and had been happy; he wanted to make me see how easy it is to fall into a job you don't like and then can't get out of because you're dependent on the salary. They all told me to 'go with your passion …'

For a while that passion was to become an inspector for the RSPCA (Royal Society for the Prevention of Cruelty to Animals), but, knowing who and what I would be dealing with, it was probably best I let go of that idea. I was possibly a bit too young and angry to hold my temper when faced with some inadequate individual who mistreats animals.

From a very early age I found some subjects at school difficult. I found mathematics and English too hard and the teacher to be cruel. I'd had enough of feeling the board rubber clout the side of my head and the chalk stinging on my cheek, so I decided to become the class jester to deflect all the bad stuff and give everyone a laugh instead. My parents could see where this was all going to end and quickly found a private tutor to help me. I was a small schoolboy with no confidence – somehow I always felt that I just wasn't good enough. These feelings of self-worth would haunt me and make unwanted reappearances throughout my adult life.

The Scouts and then the Air Training Corps hit on something with me that made a big difference to how I felt about myself. I was thirteen years old and there were people in my life, other than my sister and my wonderful parents, who believed in me. And I needed that feedback from people to know that I was on the right track. Then at seventeen years old I got a lucky break – the Air Training Corps and a lovely man called Godfrey Smith, the Commanding Officer of 768 Squadron, managed to arrange a visit to Lewisham Fire Station. This was all before health and safety regulations, so I got to go out on a shout. It was amazing and, although I didn't acknowledge it right away, the buzz of it must have been stored away in my brain. At this point I was young and headstrong and holding tight to my dream of becoming a jet pilot. The more people told me that it wasn't going to be possible, the more I stuck to my guns. In reality, I wasn't Maverick, and this wasn't *Top Gun*. With every time I watched that film I convinced myself this was going to be real life. But in real life, my dreams looked like they were fading fast because I couldn't get through the tests. Especially in maths, it felt like the numbers were having a laugh at my expense. I didn't understand why I just couldn't master it like everyone else seemed to. Everything that had held me back throughout school was coming back to halt me in my tracks again.

In my head I retained the idea of a career with the RAF, perhaps as an Air Loadmaster, a post that I had researched and thought I stood a chance at, but, as my bad luck would have it, I had chosen a job that was going to be scrapped in the next round of budget cuts, so that opportunity no longer existed. In this crazy game of snakes and ladders I was back down the longest snake.

However, the fates must have been watching me because my next move put me where I needed to be, semi-accidentally. My big decision was to take matters into my own hands and proactive: I worked and worked and worked at my maths and my English. I wasn't going to be let down by these demons, but it was an uphill struggle. Every spare minute, I wrote to airports, airfields and every fire and rescue service I could think of to see if they had any vacancies, and then I'd head back to my day job working at Sainsbury's. I just needed the experience, something on my CV that would put me above the rest. I'd send hundreds of letters but after every effort a few weeks later a letter would drop on the mat: 'Thank you but ...' To cut a long story short, I tried over and over again and three painful years later I finally received an invitation to interview for the Kent Fire Brigade. I was one in 1,000 applicants, and as I passed through each stage I had to pinch myself: it was finally happening. All the hard work was paying off – and in the end I received offer letters from three different brigades! Just like buses – nothing for ages and then three at once. I was stunned! I chose Kent and the rest, as they say, is history.

I'd made it. This was my moment. I had achieved what I truly believed in, and had finally found out who I was supposed to be. There was no going back now. I could achieve anything.

I started work on 1 April 1997 and loved everything about it: the discipline, support and being part of a team. Of course, I was always looking ahead, and I recognise that in myself now. I look as if I'm settled but I'm always aware of the next step, and the best one came to me in 2005 when I had been with the crew at Dartford Fire Station for eight years. We were a real 'band of brothers' (there were no female firefighters in the Kent Fire Brigade at the time) but I had progressed as far as I could there; it was time to make a move. And so I transferred to London, serving at Southwark Fire Station from February 2005, where among many incidents I attended the 7/7 London bombings and later received recognition for my part and actions during the harrowing incidents at Aldgate.

A mere few months later I was embarking on an adventure of a different kind, as Kate and I tied the knot. Saturday 17 September 2005 was a day to remember; the sun was shining, the sky was blue, and Kate looked absolutely stunning as she walked down the aisle. I couldn't help thinking how lucky I was to have this wonderful woman by my side. As we were leaving the church, despite having already transferred to London, my 'brothers' from Dartford were my guard of honour in full undress uniform (that's our Sunday best uniform!), forming an arch as we walked out of the church, beaming. A perfect day. Kate's been my rock ever since, and at the end of those long hard, work days, I'm so grateful to know that I can always rely on her and my girls to be there.

I was in the mood to progress. And so shortly after the wedding, I transferred again to Croydon, to see what opportunities awaited me there. Whether the rush to do so was spurred on by getting married or because after taking so long to get going on my career I didn't want to let any chances pass me by, I don't know, but I had my eyes on the accelerated promotion programme. I had managed to get to the last fifty in the selection and I only had four hurdles left to jump: a test in maths, one in English, report-writing and role play. There was only one problem – well, two problems from that list: the maths and English tests. I had my heart in my mouth sitting those papers, and I hoped that I had done enough. Hope wasn't enough, though. All I achieved was the most spectacular failure I could ever have imagined. Secretly, I knew in my heart I'd failed the tests as soon as I put my pen down – I just wanted to walk away as fast I could. I had crashed and burned and, what was worse, all my old fears returned. This disappointment had pressed all the buttons and let all those demons crawl out of the bag. I was lower than I'd been for a very long time.

But with support from Kate, I knew I had to pick myself up again and turn the failure around, because I still wanted to go for the promotion. I could compensate for my failings with the report writing and role play – by being proactive again, just like when I'd first wanted to join the Brigade, and I enrolled myself on some courses. And as for the returning demons: those I could deal with in another way. I had spent my life developing strategies for my old problems with maths and English: surely I could again? But still I really wasn't sure what was causing the problems.

I made an application to become a trainer with the London Fire Brigade and I knew that I would have to be assessed, which sent me reeling, right back to those papers I had got so wrong. There I was again, facing acceptance or rejection. I was dreading it because I was really at a stage now where I needed some positive feedback. I went ahead and enrolled on all the courses I could manage, and then a few more that put me totally out of my comfort zone. The course for dyslexia awareness sounded interesting and it turned out to be just that. It was a good course and I had no trouble completing the feedback sheet. Or at least that's what I thought. It turned out that the way I completed the form gave something away about me. My score denoted that I am dyslexic.

It was a shock to be told that at the age of thirty! But it immediately explained a great many things, including the difficulty I had with maths, and with certain aspects of reading and writing. The penny had dropped and now I was seeing myself in a whole new light. And now that help was there, maths wasn't difficult at all! The Brigade has a Learning Support Team and one of the managers, Pat Rodney, was superb in supporting me and talking me through the concerns that I had. She also put me in touch with Carol Leather, who supports people like me with declared learning needs. Carol held my hand through these initial struggles as I made sense of my diagnosis. I came to understand the missing links that I couldn't see when dealing with patterns and sequences in names and numbers was all down to my dyslexia. But break it down, look at it another way, and everything is fine. It just clicks! Simply being able to give the issue a name makes it less scary and easier to handle. Dyslexia – that was the medical term for this block that had been in my life from as long as I can remember. The diagnosis has been life-changing for me and I made sure that it *did* change my life. It was nothing to be afraid of and so I put all the awkwardness and embarrassment about my earlier 'failures' behind me. And I resolved that if either Olivia or Emma have the condition, it will be discovered early so they can get all the help they need before they suffer like I did. As a parent governor of Emma's school I can add my experience and weight to anything the school does in the way of supporting children living with dyslexia. Once you know about it, then you can work with it – everyone can work with it.

After getting my diagnosis, I wanted to talk to my mum, to thank her and Dad for all they had done to help and support me over the years. I'm not sure if they'd known dyslexia existed back then, but if they had they may well have discounted it as having nothing to do with my problems, because I was fine in other subjects. My old school reports were a good window on the past.

Looking back, I think my parents must have despaired because every knock-back made me retreat into myself a little more – to the point where I started becoming unruly.

I remember my mum saying to me in later life that some reports said I was 'disruptive and lazy'. She told them: 'What you've written here – it's not my son. I want you to give me permission to observe him in class.' She had her wish granted and she watched me, unseen, over a period of time to get her own idea of how I was behaving. Then she wrote her version of a report on me: 'This is what we think of Paul ...' and went on to describe me, her son, and not some child they labelled disruptive and lazy. It took almost twenty years or so to realise that what was happening wasn't any of that at all but something that was beyond me. I never forget to thank my mum for what she did and continues to do for me. You're my heroine. I needed to hear those words of support then, just as much as I needed to move on to the next stage of my life, and my new challenge.

I loved my job as a trainer but thanks to a Channel 4 documentary about the London Fire Brigade Fire Investigation Team I found the key to my next move. It was fixed in my brain and I was hungrier and more determined than ever. The very real and unadulterated footage of a fire station at work included the role of the Fire Investigator and I decided there and then that it was for me. Mum managed to get a copy of the programme on video, so I could watch it over and over and see what the job entailed. I really only needed to watch it once to know that was where I wanted my career to go next.

It took until 2009 to have the opportunity to apply for a Fire Investigator's job with the London Fire Brigade. That was the team I wanted to join. In the time since my dyslexia was diagnosed I have worked with educational professionals both within the Brigade and externally to better understand my particular problems and develop approaches to deal with documents that I have to produce for work, such as incident reports and reports for coroners in the case of a fatality. It's a confidence boost, that's all, but it makes me feel reassured and whole again. As for the investigator's job: that would be a timely step away from frontline firefighting, which by then I had done for twelve years. I had just become a father for the first time, so I now had Kate *and* Olivia to consider and factor into my career plans.

I applied and went through the whole process, trying my very hardest and using all the tools I had learnt over the development plan I had instigated for myself. Although seeds of doubt were always there in my mind and many said I was too young for the role, I knew what I wanted and was determined to work for it. It paid off: I succeeded and joined the elite group of Fire Investigators covering the whole of London, based on a Watch. My training was and still is the hardest, steepest learning curve I've ever undertaken in my life but the rewards were all worthwhile. I was ready for a change and a new challenge and I saw a clear pathway from firefighter to Fire Investigator, and, further down the line, I could see the way ahead to be a Dog Handler, given half the chance. This was going to be the last step I would take on my own because at the next stage of my career, there would be four more feet planted beside mine.

As for that quiet boy, he reached out for help, and this time there were people who understood, who took his hand and showed him the way. Dyslexia isn't a source of embarrassment for me: my demons have been brought out of the shadows and released. I knew from the moment that I was given the name for why I find certain things difficult that everything would start to get easier. I would need the help that had been offered, and I would take it – silly not to. Starting a new job with the weight of an old problem lifted off my shoulders felt really good. As an investigator I would be able to ask more questions about the cases, and would make good use of this promotion to work towards my ultimate goal of combining my work as a Fire Investigator with being a Fire Dog Handler. I knew where I was going from here. You don't get involved in the same way as a firefighter, saving lives and putting out fires. But the investigator's job starts with a host of questions needing answers. It felt like a fresh start: hurdles cleared and challenges met. If the frightened boy that I once was could be here right now, I'd tell him not to worry and that it's all going to be OK.

Chapter 15

Resilience in the Face of Adversity

Perhaps my struggle to join the Brigade is why I like the word 'resilience'. I've often looked it up in the dictionary to remind myself what it means: 'The ability to recover quickly from difficulties. Toughness. Spirit ...'

We talk about resilience a lot at the moment. It's an appropriate word for the Fire Brigade, and most likely for all three Emergency Services. If you can face the unpredictable and sometimes horrific, apply all your care and skills to the best of your ability, display unstinting devotion to duty and then dust yourself off and start all over again, you are tough, and you have spirit.

Strangely enough, I've never met a firefighter who thinks of himself or herself as brave, but they certainly meet a lot of people who want to call them heroes. As a firefighter I'd say I've seen a great number of my colleagues go beyond the call of duty on pure, blind instinct alone. They don't keep a tally of who did what and when, they just give the care that's needed when it is needed for a life to be saved.

The Fire Service prides itself on looking after the lost as well as the living and it wouldn't be unusual to hear me or another member of the team apologising to a fatality for having to step across them or move their body to a safer place. Is it any wonder that we are all haunted by much of what we have witnessed in our careers? I think we would need to be made of stone if we felt we had to brush off the emotional impact of dealing with death. Sherlock may not have magic powers (although some of my family and friends would disagree with me), but I'm fortunate that he does have he ability to cushion the impact of dealing with a fatality by just being there and by just being himself.

Saying that, we are all haunted by something bigger. You don't do a job like this and then walk away without getting some of it wedged under your skin. The forensic teams bag up samples of whatever Sherlock finds, and our clothes are covered in white overalls, so we don't step away with anything unless it's in our heads. One job will nudge echoes of a past case: maybe a victim of a similar age, family circumstances, a ring, a bag, a blouse ... Something will trigger a memory that will transport you to a place you didn't want to revisit. There's always somewhere, and for me it will forever be Thursday 7 July 2005.

The 7/7 terror bombings in London brought the capital's rush-hour transport system to a standstill. I was a firefighter at Southwark Fire Station, and we got the call just after the change of the Watch that morning. We had no idea of what to expect, nor what we were walking into. We were ordered to attend Aldgate Station where one of four suicide bombers had detonated an explosive on train number 204 as it entered a tunnel on the Circle Line. Descending onto the track and into the tunnel we had to work in complete darkness, feeling our way along the walls. When we reached the train, the scene that met us was something we could never have imagined. That's where I go in my nightmares even today, that tunnel. Part of me wished this was a training exercise. But this wasn't a drill. These are the days when all the things we practise are put into action. We hope we never have to face them. It's what we have to do. It wasn't until we were in the train dealing with the incident that a senior officer said that this was happening across London. Down in those tunnels, we weren't aware of the other incidents happening above ground. The Emergency Services were ordered out of the tunnel because of a likely secondary bomb, but we stayed. All of us. My own words from that day echo in my head: 'We will stay until the last saveable life has been saved.'

It's a firefighter's job to save lives. And that's what we expect to do, but when you can't, as on that day in July 2005, it's so very hard to accept. That day we couldn't save everyone because the odds were stacked against us. And that truth still haunts me.

It's part of the job to put yourself in danger – that's the occupational hazard. I try not to think about it on a normal day because I need to be out there doing my job, not wondering what could happen to me. On the morning of the bombings, we all just answered the call to attend and did everything we could do down there. The scene on the track was unreal and the smell of blood and smoke and dust was choking. We needed to free people from the wreckage and clear a way for the paramedics to reach the injured. We saw the worst and the best of humanity that day, and that will stay with me always, alongside the screams, and, more chillingly, the lack of screams ...

My world for the many hours we all worked that day was centred on what was happening in the tunnel, but I realised that close to 40 metres above me Kate would be in her office watching everything on the TV news. In a weird way she would have known more than me about what was going on. But she would see the fire engines outside the station and the ambulances waiting to transport the injured, and *not* know what was going on with me. It must have been worse for her.

After three hours or so, we emerged from underground and filled our lungs with clean air. All too aware how fortunate we were to still be alive and able to do that. Hours later when I got back to the fire station I let Kate know that I was fine. She had been worried about me, but she said, in her wonderful, stoic way, that she'd known where I was and that I would be in touch as soon as it was possible. She was, of course, right.

I can't do my job every day constantly thinking of the all-too-sobering reality that I could die. That would be foolish, and who wants to taunt fate? Whenever the 'death in service' question comes up, I always try and reassure Kate and my parents by saying: 'If it happens, it happens. Just know that I was happy.'

I know that sounds like a grim thing to say but Kate understands. We've known each other since childhood, and then we met up again after she went to university, so apart from school days she has only ever known me as a firefighter. She's familiar with the drill and you need that calm understanding from your partner, so that in a way everything is grasped without having to spelt it out – unless we want to. It's just the way life is for us because of my job. It's best that Kate doesn't think about the 'what ifs' and I certainly try not to. We both keep that little bag of anxiety well hidden.

As for the girls, they put their trust in Sherlock. They love that daft dog so much, and because he's with me all the time, Olivia and Emma have him down as their daddy's number-one protector. I think the Rockster would be very happy about that, and no doubt his broad chest would puff out all the more if he knew he was being given this special task. Emma tells him in a very calm, quiet voice that he must keep Daddy safe and be a good boy and that very clever Cocker Spaniel just sits with her and listens very intently – with his ball in his mouth.

Counselling is important for a firefighter's way of life, and I find it very useful for helping me relax more. All firefighters are offered counsellors in the Fire Brigade, but in Fire Investigation, due to the amount of fatal fires and harrowing incidents we deal with, we have biannual visits scheduled with our own counsellor. Certainly, in the aftermath of the 7/7 bombings I was grateful for someone to talk to who was understanding but at the same time impartial. Men and women in our job are not the easiest souls to search. You must scrape the surface off, go down a couple of layers and then wait to see what, if anything, seeps through. I think firefighters and investigators do the job they do because they care, and sometimes that's not always about the living. Sometimes that's caring for the lives we couldn't save. They are the ones who prey on your mind. When a firefighter attends a scene the people he or she finds are either alive or dead. Thankfully it's very rare to be in a situation where they are alive at the scene but you can't save them. When I've been on a shout involving a fatality I, like many of my colleagues, will say to the deceased, 'Rest in peace,' as if wishing the soul a safe journey to wherever it is that the soul goes. Just by being there with them a connection is made, even if it is for the briefest of moments, and you care what happens to them.

Mindfulness is also helping a lot of people in many different situations, including those serving in the Brigade, to find inner peace, and any way of achieving that is, in my mind, to be treasured. My version of mindfulness is an Insanity workout. Exercise works for me – if I'm thinking how much the exercise hurts then I'm not thinking about anything else! I'm not sure that's the kind of approach my counsellor meant, but she says if it works for me then do it. It *does* work. An hour of blistering circuits and the adrenalin and endorphins soon get the mind back on track! Ironically, this is a time Sherlock finds he can relax. There's no tail wagging, head bobbing or swaggering up and down. He has his ball and a soft toy and that's him resting. Maybe it's because he can't believe what he's seeing, and he's mesmerised! I'd go so far as to say that it works for both of us in our own ways and as long as I don't think I'm getting out of walking him then he's totally happy.

Maybe this is where that resilience comes into play again – in our work and in our downtime. Resilience defines our ability to reboot and see how much bounce-back we really have inside of us. It's working, repairing and never giving up, and being ready to face the next challenge. It's being tough but never believing you're super-human, because something will always happen to remind you that you're absolutely bloody not!

London Fire Brigade's best and brightest (L-R), Murphy, Roscoe and Sherlock.

Below: Who are you calling Fluffy? Sherlock looking much sleeker after a session with Debs, his groomer.

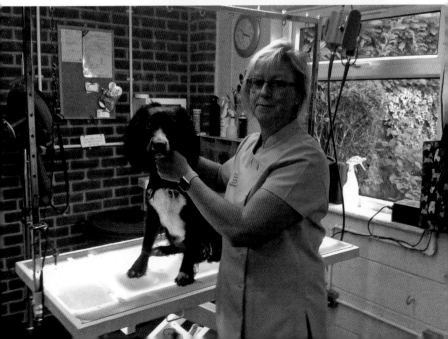

Daily Mirror and RSPCA Animal Hero Awards 2017. We already feel that Sherlock, Murphy and Roscoe are our very own heroes, but to have such public recognition is quite something.

It was a surreal experience sharing a few jokes with Richard Hammond – it's not every day you get to mingle with the stars!

One look at me in my marshmallow Tyvek® outfit and Sherlock, ears twitching and tail wagging, knows we're going to work.

Below: Sharon Fredricks drew a pastel portrait of Sherlock for the team – he's quite the icon.

Our annual Certification is always a nervy affair but as Mick always said: 'Trust your dog. Believe in him and he will lead you...'

Below: Educating the public is so important. And who is the best of all our communicators – Sherlock, of course!

Get one, test it regularly

london-fire.gov.uk

The girls and Sherlock are the greatest of friends – even when Sherlock is pretending to be a show pony in their imagination games.

Below: All that digging means that Sherlock can't escape the dreaded bath!

Having my family beside me when I was presented with the Long Service and Good Conduct Medal to mark my twenty years in the Fire Service was the best feeling in the world.

Right: Assistant Commissioner Dan Daly presenting Sherlock and me with a Borough Commanders Letter of Congratulations for all of our efforts at Fire Station open days marking the 150th anniversary of the London Fire Brigade.

Don't be fooled by the innocent eyes – I've just munched my way through the Christmas gingerbread house.

Above: Meeting HRH the Prince of Wales was an absolute honour. I love this photograph as it looks like Sherlock is being knighted!

Sir David Amess MP, with his work on the advisory group for fire safety, has been very supportive. It was fantastic to show him just how brilliant Sherlock is on our visit to Parliament.

Above: The London Fire Brigade 150th Anniversary Special Edition *Monopoly* dog counter based on Sherlock! © Hasbro.

FIRE INVESTIGATION

DOG TEAM

DIESEL

Rockster, Wonder Dog, Sherlock:
truly this man's best friend.

Chapter 16

At Home with the Osbornes

I think 'resilient' describes Sherlock perfectly too. He had a good start in life and he has been loved and cared for ever since, but when he had trouble with his leg I thought we could lose him as a working dog. Yet he bounced back, good as new and twice as naughty, and returned to his duties at work and at home. As he has grown into the fabric of our family life, Sherlock is getting used to spending more time in the house, so he sees more of the girls and I like that he wants to be with us. As Kate said when he arrived, he is our third baby. He's certainly the naughtiest 'child' in the house, that's for sure, but he has a lovely habit of delivering his naughtiness with a cuteness that makes it almost impossible to be angry with him. Almost!

I'm not sure I saw this part of the story coming when Sherlock first arrived in our lives because there's no way he could be described as a normal family pet. He's too much of a working dog for that. He knows that when that harness goes on and I'm in my work wear we're on duty, and somewhere along the line that's going to mean a trip in the van and a search. He must sense the change in my body language when I'm in uniform because I sense the same in him. It's the same again when I pull on the white forensic suit ahead of a search. I can feel a more focused Sherlock at the end of the lead. And when I release him to search it's as if he is drawing on every atom of energy from every corner of his body and concentrating it on the task.

That's, of course, alongside the other duties that the girls give him. Such as how after school Emma likes to re-enact her day, and that usually includes creating a classroom scene, lining up her toys – and Sherlock – to represent her classmates. He's very good with her and plays along perfectly. I'm always surprised when I hear that he hasn't spent all the time on the naughty step. And it turns out that he can be very obliging in a game of *My Little Pony* too! I'm not sure if Emma is a budding thespian but she loves to act out scenes, and sometimes, when she's not playing teacher, the conservatory or the garden becomes an imaginary extension of something akin to the Spanish Riding School! Most of the action is naturally in Emma's head, but because Sherlock is the nearest thing we have to a pony in the Osborne household, he often finds himself being trotted around the garden like a Lipizzaner prancing and dancing show horse! He's there, on a lead-rein (his own lead), giving it all the moves, clearly following instructions to hold his head higher and 'trot on'. It really is a bit of magic. Kate and I simply howl with laughter sometimes because this dog is so special: one minute a playmate to Emma and Olivia and the next a tip-to-toe professional out with me on a fatality shout.

After a harrowing incident I always come home and I hug everyone that little bit tighter, and share more of my time and head-space with my family, appreciating every second in the company of those I love and who love me. And who's sitting proudly, eyes shining and tail wagging, right in the middle of us? Our dog, Sherlock.

Now, I'd hate anyone to think that Sherlock's ability to swap from working wonder dog to puppy playmate has happened overnight. This boy has had to earn his stripes. There was one Osborne family outing the summer that Sherlock came to us, when everyone was enjoying a Mr Whippy cone from the ice-cream van – except for

Sherlock. I saw him looking at our ice creams and probably wondering when he was going to get a little try, but I thought nothing of it. He's a dog and it's what dogs do. But dogs are also born opportunists and that day we made a Sherlock-sized mistake! As Emma turned towards me so I could wipe her face, Sherlock saw his moment to dip down and nick her ice cream clean out of its cone! Oh boy, was he quick! He had the speed and accuracy of one of those cheeky seagulls on Brighton Pier, but he did it with pure grace and style. We were a bit more careful with ice cream number two!

And who could forget the bunnies? Olivia loves her rabbits Flopsy and Luca – and so does Sherlock. I wasn't sure if we could trust Sherlock around real rabbits after his kidnap and attempted burial of her soft toy rabbit Bunny soon after he arrived, but Olivia had been promised two bunnies for her sixth birthday and I had to keep that promise. I didn't get much chance to forget – my daughter reminded me every single week for three years! So, was I apprehensive about the rabbit idea? Yes, but only because I had made the promise pre-Sherlock and I wasn't sure how he would react. Mick summed it up pretty well when he said to me: 'Good luck! A dog with a retriever instinct and two fluffy bunnies. Could spell disaster!'

A promise is a promise, so happy birthday, Olivia, and hello to Flopsy and Luca, two dwarf lop-eared rabbits. Sherlock said hello in his own way by shadow chasing them around and around their circular metal run. He was getting a bit too enthusiastic for my liking but after some straight talking he learnt that they weren't a new toy and ever since then all he does is lie next to them, very quietly, with the bars of the run between them! I'm not sure if I would trust him to be alone with them but I think we have an understanding and there haven't been any close calls – yet.

There have been times when I've described Sherlock as 'quite a handful' and have let others fill in the gaps. He's not really a naughty dog; at least, I don't think he is. What he is is full of energy and it needs a dog with Sherlock's level of drive and personality to do the job we do. It's when the drive and personality in the work dog overlap with the world of the loveable rogue who's auditioning for the role of 'pet' that sparks fly! It's one of the reasons why he always ends up finishing the night of a family party or BBQ tied to the table. He looks at the spread of food and his eyes say: 'Oh, thank you very much. Well, that's me sorted. What are the rest of you having?' And from that moment on he just can't sit still. He has that 'dog on a mission' look about him and

I guess it's one of the benefits of having a pretty face and knowing all the doggy-charm tricks in the book that he can work the room and beg all he can. Plates left on Sherlock-level are investigated and demolished and moments of boredom are filled with spells of digging in the garden and then returning to the party looking like the Creature from the Black Lagoon – plus mud-plastered nose and paws. Muddy dog – the ideal party guest. Not! As soon as I hear the words: 'Paul, can you do something with Sherlock?' I know that my partner in crime has let the side down.

I can usually find him on food-watch – that's if he's not 'mingling' and getting in the way. The trouble is he's the wrong height for a party. At about knee-height, he can be a dark, swirling mass of invisibility that you don't see until he trips you over. As his tail is a force of nature all on its own, it can send trays of nibbles scattering and in no time at all Sherlock is the centre of attention – but not in a good way. One look from Kate and I know that it's over to me to sort things out before we're all treading on peanuts and party food.

'Sherlock ... over here, mate. There's a good lad. So ... what are you up to?' He always comes to me right away and we have one of our man-to-dog chats. 'OK, this is the moment where I say you're on table duty or it's back to your kennel. Which is it going to be?' I know he hates being in his kennel when there's something more exciting going on – after all, if he wanted to be in there he could wander in and out as he liked. 'Righto, the table it is, mate. And at least we know where you are and what you're doing!' Once on the lead he takes on a semi-working stance and sits in an almost military 'to attention' pose. He's taking it all in but not taking anyone out!

In the summer in particular he loves to be outdoors. Maybe he'll lie in the kitchen on the cool floor for a while but then he'll want to be outside. (Actually it's the same whatever the season, come hail, wind, snow or rain.) But being the contrary creature that he can be, if we are all sitting in the conservatory and he is in the garden he will start pacing. First of all, he begins by walking up and down in front of where we are sitting. He'll glance inside several times as he picks up the pace. If he's still being ignored, then the situation calls for a slow trot, which he will repeat a handful of times before he really cranks up the speed and breaks into a full-on jog! It's as if he's limbering up for a big race, with lots of exaggerated moves. Of course, we are all dying to burst out laughing but it's more fun to see how far he will go to get our attention. Toys, that's the next thing, and he has quite a choice, so we're always intrigued which one he'll choose to catch our eye. Naturally it's one of the smellier ones that he's had 'fermenting' in his kennel. He buries them in the garden first, then digs them up according to his own little rota and chews them a bit, then returns them to the earth, ready to repeat. I can see Kate's pulling a face as soon as she sees Sherlock's weapon of choice. She's not going to want that trailed into the house – it's green and looks like it will smell like the devil.

We're talking and eating, and the girls are showing us some drawings and so just for a moment we're not watching Sherlock – and clearly he sees that we are ignoring him. Well, that won't do so it's time for his party piece. 'Oh, look, Daddy, Sherlock's playing the piano!' Emma is watching our daft dog stand on his hind legs, putting his paws on the window sill of the conservatory and working his way around the sill, plonking his paws up and down. It really does look as if he's playing the piano! Then I notice the colour of his paws. Digging up his slimy thing to chew and doing his own version of 'show and tell' has left him with mud clogging up his paws, which are now running up and down the white sills leaving very muddy footprints!

Not one to take even a heavy hint, Sherlock clearly still fancies his chances of joining us in the conservatory and getting some food and a bit of fuss. I ask him, 'Have you seen yourself, Sherlock? You look like a mud dog – you don't stand a cat's chance in hell of being allowed in here with us looking like that. But you're not bad on the piano, mate, I'll give you that.'

Then comes the sulk. He knows what I'm saying and I'm saying it in the usual calm voice that I use with him at work, so he realises I mean it, and consequently he drifts off ... If only he hadn't gone and covered himself in all that mud! It's a lovely afternoon – the daft dog could have joined us. Never mind, I'll catch up with him in a minute – after he's buried that slimy mess.

'Daddy? Have you seen Sherlock?'

'No, sweetheart, he's somewhere in the garden. He's OK.'

'Yes, Daddy, he's OK but he's not in the garden. He's on the sofa and he's got that green thing with him ... Oh Sherlock, you're so naughty!'

Sherlock has most definitely become part of our family traditions and therefore part of us. Last Christmas we did all the usual things: went to the pantomime, church for a carol concert, watched some Christmas films, and then there's always the best performance of the festive season – me playing Michael Bublé while singing along (badly!). One of the new things that Kate has added to our traditions list of is the making of (from scratch) a gingerbread house complete with gingerbread snowmen, people, trees and coconut-flake snow.

Christmas Eve is a big day for us and this year's walk was lovely but cold and we were happy to get home and snuggle in with a hot drink and a Christmas film. We were all tired, Sherlock included, so he got to stay in his favourite spot in the kitchen while the rest of us were in the lounge. Kate had brought in our drinks, closing the front-room door behind her. Now, she often leaves the kitchen door open, not meaning to, so I'm the boring one shouting: 'Have you shut the kitchen door?' and getting the good old roll of the eyes treatment and that little 'huff' of 'of course I have'. This was one of those moments, but there was some hesitation: 'It's all right,' Emma assured me, 'I've taught Sherlock not to go upstairs.' I doubted that very much but decided not to be a grump and left it to the spin of chance: fifty-fifty open door and Sherlock up to no good or Sherlock behind a closed door and no problems.

Note to self: never leave things to chance where Sherlock is concerned. 'SHERLOCK … SHERLOCK, WHERE ARE YOU?' Kate may have left the room but I knew from her tone that he was on the loose somewhere in the house and there were too many terrible possible scenarios to consider: had he discovered the soft toy pile, or the Christmas presents wrapped and ready to give out? Please God, don't let them have been chewed and slobbered on or ripped apart for the food inside. But Kate had seen something worse ...

... The kitchen door was open, Sherlock's toy was abandoned on the threshold to the hallway, and there was no Sherlock to be seen or ... heard. The next words were Kate's: 'Sherlock ... no!' These words were followed by a scrabbling of kids' feet from the front room to see what the commotion was all about, and a scrabbling of claws on a wooden floor wherever Wonder Dog was trying to flee from. I checked myself: I did ask if the door into the kitchen was closed, didn't I? Thank goodness I didn't say it out loud because there was Kate, open-mouthed – and not happy. She had been greeted with the sight of Sherlock in the conservatory with what was left of the gingerbread house. It had been left at perfect Sherlock height – level with his mouth on the coffee table. Using my investigative skills, I deduced that he had tiptoed from the kitchen through the dining room and in through the open door to the conservatory. It was like the Sherlock version of Cluedo!

The coconut shavings were everywhere including in Sherlock's beard – number one clue to his guilt. Clue number two: one end of the house no longer had a dusting of icing sugar: it was back to bare biscuit and very … wet! Sherlock had cleaned the walls of the house very neatly, hoovering up the coconut snow. And something was missing. The final clue to Sherlock's sugar-rush robbery was the disappearance of some important people: the Christmas tableau was short of gingerbread snowmen, trees and people. Yes, Sherlock had eaten them. It wasn't going to need my pals from CID to solve this case.

'Resilience' is the word for sure. Whoever thought of that word which pops up frequently in job specs, PR material and Brigade literature had it spot on. You really do need to have the flexibility to take knocks and bounce back in order to meet the next situation and give your best.

I can tell you, Kate too needed a whole lot of resilience that day!

Chapter 17

Back to School

Sherlock and I can never rest on our laurels. Every year Sherlock and I have to prove that we deserve our licence to practise with the Brigade by passing through the Certification process. It's also a good opportunity to train with Clive, who is responsible for keeping us up to speed with the new theories and practical techniques we need to do our job to the highest standard. Of course, I already know that I can rely on my faithful dog to do his stuff. I know that he is used to getting full marks every year and every year my chest puffs out with pride when I take that certificate in my hand and look at Sherlock sitting at my feet ... munched-up tennis ball in his mouth and wearing that sparkly-eyed expression on his handsome face.

Sherlock's first Certification was a very stressful moment for me, although not for Sherlock because His Majesty just thought it was just another day out and a chance to have some fun. Quite a different story for me. It took place, as it has done every year since, at the Fire Service College in Moreton-in-Marsh, Gloucestershire, and works similarly to our graduation tests with Clive. We'd practised and practised the different disciplines. Our first search was conducted on the lead, going along a line of eight gallon-sized paint tins with holes drilled in the tops to allow the scent of the various burnt items inside them, ranging from rubber to plastic to wood, to escape. In one, there had been an ignitable liquid, which had been burnt. Sherlock needed to identify the substance and I needed to identify his 'hit', then drop the lead, walk away and call it in as an identification of his target substance. Same again with the items of clothing arranged in a line, with me holding Sherlock on his lead. Next came the large building search, off the lead, in a lecture theatre; then a small set of rooms, followed by a large open-area search covering a sector 500 metres square, through woodland and grassland.

The first search for the Certification had to impress the assessor, Stuart Holder, who'd never seen me before and didn't know Sherlock, so we had a lot of ground to make up and everything to prove. He's a granite wall of a man, tough, northern, and not a chap I'd welcome a right hook from in a disagreement. This was the man who would decide if we had achieved competence and whether we would qualify as a team. What if he decided we didn't pass muster? I'd heard stories of dogs and handlers not being up to standard and I really didn't want to be in that camp.

OK … this was it. First the run along the tins: 'It's a blank, sir,' I say. He looked at me closely, poker-faced. I froze. Oh shit, I think Sherlock missed it! No, remember … Mick and Clive told me: 'Trust your dog.' But the look Stuart gave me suggested I'd missed something. Bugger! First task and I've cocked up. I heard Stuart call for the next dog to come forward. There were three of us going up for the Certification trophy today. So began the merry-go-round of handlers, but the one thing we couldn't do was observe what the others were doing. It's best that way but it's still stressful, because we can't help seeing each other as competition. The other handler came back from his first task: 'Yep. Got it on the first tin!' he said, chuffed to pieces.

Now I felt really low. The other guy's confidence had shaken my own. I needed to do better next time. I got called for a second attempt. All the time, I kept repeating the same words over and over in my head: 'Trust your dog, Paul. Trust your dog ...' I was told before I started that I would have another chance. I seized it and as I progressed along the tins – nothing. I told Stuart that we'd hit upon another blank again. Then he looked at me, not giving anything away and coolly asked me if I wanted another go.

'No, sir, thank you. I'm trusting my dog here.' I said it but deep inside I was doubting us big time. The thing is Sherlock was looking very cool and calm and collected. He was very much Sherlock at the top of his game – but then he always is. I think all the anxiety was coming from me. He didn't know this situation was so crucial – only I knew that. The other handler had this turn, but said to me that he'd buckled and asked for another go. That told me right away that he didn't trust his dog. He had pushed his dog on to something that wasn't there. Bad luck.

I went up again. We had another chance to prove what we were capable of to Stuart. He wasn't going to make it easy for us and so he set up a new arrangement of tins. Sherlock's body was taut, and I could tell he was totally focused, locked in. There was only concentration on his face and determination in every step and sniff. We started along the tins ... 1, 2, 3, 4, 5, 6 ... aaaaggghhhhh ... Then 7 ... bang! He stuck his nose to it! 'Bloody hell!'

were the first words I heard and they came from Stuart's direction. I walked away, but Sherlock stayed. He was waiting for his reward – his beloved tennis ball.

'That's one indication for his target substance, sir,' I said.

Stuart looked amazed by what Sherlock had just done: 'I can see why you were so cocksure of yourself now! That dog is amazing. Bang on both times! It's absolutely superb work to have that much trust between you. That's a team. Well done.' We'd only just started, and we were on fire.

The day progressed well. Sherlock was the best I've ever seen him. Although I said that he could have had no idea how important that day was to us, it was as if he was totally aware of its significance. There was no messing about and no hesitation, but then that's Sherlock all over. It was just incredible that he drew on everything he had ever been taught and harnessed every shred of concentration he possessed. He was like a search machine! The way Sherlock was for me that day was better than I could ever have imagined, and the look on Stuart's face said it all. We received a glowing report and I was beyond happy. My boss Charlie and the rest of my management were happy too, but I sensed a lack of enthusiasm which was a bit annoying, so I had to ask what was wrong.

'But, Paul, it's you and Sherlock. If you hadn't been outstanding and you hadn't achieved a glowing report, then we would have thought there was something wrong! You obviously don't realise that we have expectations when it comes to you two: we expect you to deliver. But if you want to hear it anyway ... well done! We knew that you'd achieve all that was asked of you.'

Maybe I should never have doubted us. Maybe I didn't. It was just that making it meant so much to me. I didn't want to fail and if Sherlock picked up on anything that day it was my absolute determination to succeed. We hadn't come this far to be knocked back. I knew what Sherlock was capable of and I knew what we could do together, so all we needed to do was make it happen.

Maybe in those moments of doubt the seven-year-old boy who struggled at school had made a return visit. He had worked his way up to the surface once again, as happens every so often when I find myself in times of doubt and challenge. I started to hear the old voices: 'You can't do that. You'll fail. That's not something you can do. Face it, Paul, that's not for you ...' All those old insecurities coming in to eat away at me. But this time was different. I kept those thoughts at bay, and I had my champion at my side. They could not have known that even if I had my niggling doubts, Sherlock didn't care for a single one. He had enough strength and confidence for the two of us! I wasn't alone in this quest. I had Sherlock – and he had me.

'Sherlock, what on earth have you done with that monkey?' I had to ask the question because I knew that he'd had it, and it was just a matter of finding out what he had done with it. The day had started really well. We were visiting my parents and I wanted them to see this star of a dog. I was so proud of how well he had done in his Certification the previous day, but half of my brain was worried how Sherlock would hit it off with my mum's whippet, Tilly, and Dad's Dachshund, called Jack. Tilly liked Sherlock instantly; Jack viewed him with suspicion, so the room was divided but peace prevailed – well, just about. The only possible bone of contention was a PG Tips monkey toy that was lying in no man's land.

'Paul, let Sherlock have it. The other two aren't bothered really and you can tell that he wants it.' They were Mum's famous last words, marking the last that was seen of the monkey.

No one gave Monkey a second thought until it was time for us to leave. 'OK, Sherlock, you can hand Monkey over now. Time to go.' All the time I was speaking I was looking for the toy, which seemed to have done a disappearing act. Sherlock was looking very sheepish but there was no sign of anything having been chewed and dismantled – no shreds of material or severed limbs. Nothing. In minutes we were all looking for traces of Monkey. Even Tilly joined in 'looking', and she did seem to have a hot lead on it, but in the end we were all running around in circles and there was nothing to be found. I was afraid that Sherlock had buried the thing somewhere and it would be ruined forever; worse than that, if he had swallowed Monkey we were in for a whole lot of trouble. The thing is the toy looked a bit like a sock – and Sherlock loved socks ... but not in a healthy way.

A day went by and nothing 're-emerged'. I decided to take Sherlock to the vet just in case Monkey was stuck inside him as so many socks had been before. It wasn't clear whether there was anything in there but Sherlock was perfectly happy and wasn't showing signs of anything being wrong. He wasn't quiet and withdrawn or showing any pain. But I wasn't convinced all was well. I kept a close eye on everything that he was passing – knowing I couldn't miss the appearance of a small stuffed toy! Nothing.

It must have been about two weeks later that I noticed a strange smell in Sherlock's kennel. That wasn't unusual in itself, but this smell had a particularly ghastly quality about it, so I decided to take a good look around to see what was to blame. I lifted the corner of his duvet and there he was – Monkey! I was so damned pleased to see that toy. Although it was a shadow of its former self and covered in slime, grass and mud, moulded into a putty-coloured sausage, it was definitely Monkey – just the sicked-up version. It turned out that, like many a sock before him, Monkey had been chewed and swallowed before getting lodged on a 'shelf' above Sherlock's stomach. Thankfully he hadn't made the journey into Sherlock's digestive system, because if he had, I think it would have created a big problem. Sherlock really had bitten off more than he could chew (and pass) this time but miraculously he escaped surgery. I didn't think Mum would want Monkey back, but I knew that she would be pleased that Monkeygate, as it came to be known in the family, was over.

Chapter 18

Lending a Helping Paw ...

O ur work doesn't always end when the fire crew leaves and Sherlock goes back in the van; sometimes we get to see a long-term positive outcome that is far-reaching, way beyond our home patch. Meeting people living in the London community is a very special part of what we do. It's the 'hearts and minds' projects that I enjoy the most, because when you engage face-to-face with people you have the best chance of getting your message across and making a difference. And in our line of work, reaching out with our message can save lives. Fire prevention bridges all political, cultural and religious divisions because safety is in everyone's interests. We all want to protect our family.

The London Fire Brigade has a big patch to cover so everyone has to get involved with staff at each of the hundred or so stations, getting into the local community to raise awareness of fire safety and prevention through visits to community groups, local and national charity-fundraising groups, sheltered accommodation and student communities, schools and academies. You name it and the Brigade will be in touch with it in some way, shape or form. In some areas it will be a historical connection dating back to the times when all towns and even some villages had their own fire engine and volunteer crew. The fire-station building may still exist, its height and big, wide doors a dead giveaway, even if the engine and crew have long gone, a sign that the Fire Brigade remains part of the community.

We in the London Fire Brigade, as other brigades all over the country, don't support a specific charity, but a whole range. Each year a team of around thirty from the Brigade takes part in the London Marathon with each individual running to raise money for at least one charity, the causes ranging from dementia to cancer to disabilities and covering all age groups, in addition to our own Fire Fighters Charity, which assists all of us, when and if we need it. In 2009, the year that Olivia was born, I ran the London Marathon as one of the Brigade team and raised valuable money for the Royal National Institute for the Blind (RNIB) as well as for Guide Dogs. My nan was helped by the RNIB and their support team during her later years, as her eyesight deteriorated and she could no longer see. They would send her audio books and help her manage living without her sight, and so running the Marathon was my opportunity to run in her memory and give back to the organisation. I completed it in 4 hours and 22 minutes and was extremely proud to have raised over £1,000 for an incredible charity that makes such a difference.

Alongside pounding the pavement, I get to open a few doors into the community because I work with a great communicator – probably the best in the business when it comes to breaking down barriers: a dog.

Sherlock is popular wherever we show up, and we show up in lots of different places to meet people of all ages and from diverse cultural backgrounds. It's true that not everyone can be expected to be dog-friendly, and I would never force anyone to meet Sherlock. Common issues usually lie with the parents saying their child doesn't like dogs or is scared of them, which is understandable if they have had a bad experience with a dog in the past. It can take some time to overcome the fear of that happening all over again, even if you're meeting an entirely different dog. What we often find – and it's lovely when this happens – is that when children meet Sherlock, a change takes place. Over the years, I've seen children who arrive thinking they are afraid of dogs, and leave us in love with them – or at least in love with Sherlock!

Sherlock, like all the Fire Dogs, is a passive character. He's a sniffer dog so he doesn't need to have the aggressive streak of a guard or patrol dog. But he's still a dog in uniform, and if people's experience of other working dogs is one trained to carry out crowd control or protection work, then I can understand why they would hesitate to approach him, but Sherlock's discipline requires him to have a quiet and placid nature with a strong urge to do the job he does. That's really all Sherlock is interested in most of the time – doing his search job for me and getting a treat for doing it.

One child arrived at an open day with his mum who explained how terrified her son was of dogs. By the end of our time, there the little chap was practically hanging from Sherlock's neck and didn't want to leave! Tears were shed, and it was a shame it had to be like that, but he was happy about meeting Sherlock, his mum was happy that he had enjoyed himself and overcome a fear (whether it was the boy's fear or her own), and they could go away and follow Sherlock's antics on Facebook. That's a good side of social media, and it works for children because Sherlock is their link with the London Fire Brigade's fire-safety messaging too. He is a dog and he is a real detective, just like his namesake, which makes them want to share in all he gets up to, and so, without realising it, they learn a lot about the Brigade too.

Sherlock has helped many grown-ups face their fears too. Sometimes people have spent their entire lifetime harbouring an ingrained fear of dogs because a dog scared them once upon a time. If you're the one that feels it, that fear is very real. But it's a pity that same fear applies to *all* dogs. Since I've been working with Sherlock as a dog handler I've seen frightened people spend time with him, enjoy stroking him and talking to him, and then in a short space of time have their sometimes long-held negative fear of dogs turned into pure enjoyment of a dog's company. I've seen Sherlock change people's lives that way – right in front of my eyes. Now if that isn't a little bit of magic, I don't know what is. That's another feather in his cap. Well, it would be if he had a cap!

Conquering a fear of any kind is a massive step in anyone's life – I know that from personal experience. Breaking free of the ties that bind you and hold you back in anything in your life is massively positive. Only then are you free to accept all the new experiences that can take you forward. One thing is for sure – fear is responsible for more failures than lack of skill. I know that because I've experienced the pain of not believing in myself, but then I turned that around by fixing my hopes, self-belief and energy on what I wanted and where I saw myself.

It's the most heart-warming thing to see children believe in themselves and eager to follow their dreams, and it's so important to harness their influence on change and progress. I know we can't teach common sense, but when we share stories of people doing silly things and causing fires and risking lives, some lessons will be learnt. Incidents such as someone using a toilet roll as a candle holder (with the candle alight)! Or attempting to dry out a loo roll in the microwave! They are ridiculous, but they happen because some people don't think about what they're doing.

If we can impart our knowledge about fire safety to children, then there's every chance that we can reduce the number of accidents in the home that involve fire. Sherlock comes into my Year 1 talks where we cover 'senses' and their relation to fire safety. We talk about how he uses his acute sense of smell and why he can do his job so well because his nose is much better than a human's. The children like to know that Sherlock is the best at his job! He of course comes into his own showing off his collection of leads for different types of work and walking around in his little boots. The boys and girls get to try on my Watch Manager's white helmet and all of that kind of thing, but what they like most of all is Sherlock. And who knows? We could be talking to some firefighters of tomorrow ...

My daughters' school also runs a forest school which allows the children to engage with the great outdoors over a six-week period and build things working in teams. It's like a mini-leadership course, and all the time they are learning valuable life lessons without really knowing it. The session ends on the sixth week with toasting marshmallows or bread over a campfire. This gives me the perfect opportunity to discuss fire, the Fire Triangle and fire science, and also the dangers of fire, and what to do if someone's clothes catch alight, and how to call the Emergency Services. It doesn't spoil their enjoyment of their marshmallows because the children are fascinated.

With Year 2 children I run a session on the Great Fire of London, and re-enact it, building London from cardboard boxes filled with straw. We put them together and talk about fire dynamics and why the fire was so destructive. We're talking about something that is so visual and so scary that it's bound to capture their imaginations. It's all stirring stuff. I love it and the children love hearing it. I never see any glazed expressions, and besides, if they're not looking at me I know that they will be looking at Sherlock. If it's a session with Sherlock present you know that it's an experience they won't forget.

The London Fire Brigade schools drive includes working with groups of children on the autistic spectrum and offering a practical day of activities that everyone can get involved in. Although Sherlock isn't around for all the school visits, when he is you see that magic he can generate. It just takes a dog to make an appearance and you have something very special indeed.

One of the most inspiring places I recommend families to visit is the Brigade's pop-up museum. I can't help but smile at the excitement and ambition of the children learning about the history of the Brigade, as they are inspired by the brave men and women who I am proud to call my colleagues. For example, the exhibition dedicated to Women in the Fire Service sheds light on a little-known aspect of the Brigade's history and dashes any preconceived ideas about the Service only being for men who can climb tall ladders and throw people over their shoulders to rescue damsels in distress from burning buildings! It's not like that at all and, in fact, it never has been like that. Women have been in the Service carrying out administrative jobs and non-operational tasks since the First World War (1914–18) but really came into their own in the Second World War (1939–45). While their male counterparts were exempt from military service, as the Fire Service was a reserved occupation, additional numbers came from the recruitment of auxiliary firefighters and women who all helped to keep the fires at home under control. As Hitler did his best to destroy London with bombs and fire, the Brigade, alongside an army of civilians, fought to keep the capital safe.

I see little girls, particularly, looking at the photographs of the young women of the Brigade's wartime Messenger Service on their motorbikes: they smile and are obviously imagining how exciting that must have been, especially during a time when it would have been unusual to see a girl on a motorbike in peacetime. And now we have Commissioner Dany Cotton leading the way as the first woman to hold the top position in the Brigade's 150-year history.

What's good for the Service and for Sherlock is that the Commissioner is a self-confessed dog lover with a huge understanding of and belief in the Fire Investigation Dogs. I remember Mick Boyle advising me not to leave Sherlock alone with her because I would never see him again! He based this on the day he was involved in a media event with Roscoe and Murphy and the Commissioner asked for the dogs to be brought to her office, where they were discovered, much later, having a great time playing ball and being spoilt! I think the future of the Dog Team will be safe in her hands.

These days, as the Fire Dogs are gaining more publicity, we are receiving more invitations to attend charity events, and as long as everyone can accommodate a dog then we are usually happy to go along and support. We often visit the older members of the community, and Sherlock is always the star of the show. Memories of pets loved and lost over the years often come flooding back, with Sherlock being the focus of all the fuss and the love that goes with that special pet memory. He can take all of that, all afternoon. As long as he knows I'm going to take him for a run after all the work then he's happy to be the obedient Fire Dog. Well, usually he is …

I've never forgotten Dave telling me about Sherlock's first appearance for charity, which was a 'meet and greet' event for Age UK. He was still a puppy and had not started any of his training, so he was being his puppy self while Dave's Fire Dog, Sam, showed him the ropes. Knowing Sherlock as I do now I would say he was probably in his own little bubble – where he goes to when he's minding his own business and no one else's – which must have been why he decided to have a wee up the side of a resident's mattress! I can imagine Dave was a bit embarrassed and I think the Brigade probably had to pay for a new mattress, so not the greatest charity debut for the Rockster!

Not Sherlock's greatest moment, but since then Sherlock's been working on his manners. The one charity event Sherlock and I personally try to attend each year is the Starlight charity's summer party for seriously and terminally ill children. Starlight's work is so humbling; it makes your heart hurt just to read about some of the children. Children shouldn't be robbed of their future, that's not fair, and as I'm a dad it hurts on that level too. I can't imagine how I would feel if I had to face such a thing with either of my girls.

Daisy Nimmo was born with a rare genetic condition that had made her very sick all her twelve years of life. When she wasn't at home with her loving family she was a patient of Great Ormond Street Hospital in London, but Daisy's condition made every day that little bit more uncertain. Daisy had a therapy dog called Pluto to help make her life a little easier. Also a spaniel, Pluto was always there for her, helping to calm Daisy when she was stressed, licking her face when she had a seizure until it passed, and walking by her wheelchair to comfort her. One day, Daisy and her mum Stephanie saw an article about the Fire Dogs, working dogs just like Pluto, and were so excited about what we were doing. Daisy loved following Sherlock's adventures on social media so Stephanie knew that Daisy would love, more than anything, to meet and help train one of the Fire Dogs. This was definitely a job for Sherlock.

Over the time it took to make the day happen we got to know more about Daisy and what a happy girl she was, despite the challenges of her condition. So, it was so great to be able to organise something special for her.

Daisy didn't know anything about what we'd been planning, so on the day Sherlock and I went into her school to surprise her, where we took her out of the classroom so that she could spend some time with Sherlock. Stephanie was out walking Pluto at the time, and after receiving a call saying that we were there, she raced over to the school to find Daisy and her carer with us, Daisy very happily holding court with Sherlock. Sherlock's energy can be a little overwhelming, but she showed no signs of fear with him, and her wheelchair didn't perturb him at all – he even put his front paws up on it at one point to say hello! We were going to put Sherlock through his paces as a training exercise, so Daisy and I went around an outside area and she chose the locations of the hides. To distract Sherlock for a while the firefighters showed Daisy around the fire engine, but soon it was Sherlock's time to shine. He raced around at his usual speed, indicating at each spot. Daisy was in charge of delivering Sherlock's reward, so when he correctly indicated on a target substance, Daisy would throw the ball as close to his nose as possible. Sherlock normally looks to me for his reward, so with Daisy helping me it was as if the ball appeared by magic – and she was a dab hand at it too. Our day together was brilliant fun, and Sherlock was very much on his best behaviour and let Daisy fuss over him as much as she liked – which was a lot! What was heartbreaking was that I remember Daisy asking for her dad. Daisy had lost her father, Andy, to cancer the year before and, from talking to Stephanie, this had had a major impact on the family but especially on Daisy. That cut me up but made me realise even more why it's so important that despite how busy we are, we should always be generous to others. What was a small gesture from us meant so much to Daisy.

Sadly, just a short time after her day with us, Daisy lost her fight for life and slipped away in the presence of her mum and her brothers and sister. Stephanie said in a letter: 'Please thank everyone at LFB. She was your biggest fan and I will always smile whenever I see a fire engine. Sherlock is the most amazing dog. I'm so glad she met him.' Sherlock had made Daisy's dream come true.

Chapter 19

150 Years in the Making

How do you prepare a dog to meet a prince? You don't. While the rest of us were busy polishing the fire engines, scrubbing the yard and brushing up our No. 1 dress uniforms, the coolest customer for miles around was Sherlock.

The occasion was the royal opening of the new fire station in Shadwell to celebrate the London Fire Brigade's 150th anniversary in 2016. The visit was going to mark the opening of a new chapter in Shadwell's history, having had a fire station on the site since 1937, and before that a parish water pump in St Paul's Churchyard, so it was wonderful that the new state-of-the-art fire station would be welcoming the future in the presence of royalty.

Naturally, Sherlock had been to see his groomer, Debs, for a last-minute bath and smooth-over so that he was at his sweet-smelling and shiny best before meeting His Royal Highness the Prince of Wales. We didn't know until the day before who the VIP would be, but I had hoped it would be a member of the royal family. All I had to do was keep Sherlock looking smart for a morning and we would be home and dry.

I had a feeling Sherlock was going to be the main attraction. Not just because the royals are such self-confessed dog lovers but because Sherlock always makes his presence felt. He may do a good impression of being shy, but he can pull off a right regal stance if the occasion requires! When it comes to any big occasion, he allows himself to lap up the attention.

I'm sure he could tell there was something different about that day from the moment I went to wake him up that morning. 'You OK, mate? Special day for us, so we need to get out for our walk and then get you all washed and brushed up. You're going to meet a prince, so no dirty paws allowed!'

It was a good morning to run into his mate Ike, an ex-police spaniel who was out for his morning constitutional in the park too, because I needed Sherlock to get rid of some energy but not to get muddy! Having sorted out their differences some time ago, I knew they'd be happy to just play, giving me time to have a think about what I was going to say to His Royal Highness, if I was given the chance.

Lots of preparation goes into a royal visit, but for security reasons it's not something you can tell people about. The station was a hive of activity and excitement when we got to Shadwell. With so much going on I was pleased that Sherlock was keeping himself amused and staying out of the way in his kennel while everyone else rushed around getting the station and themselves ready. I'll admit to having been a wee bit nervous about the visit, but only because I wanted Sherlock to behave himself. A part of me *knew* that he could behave perfectly; it was just the other part of me, the part that knew exactly what devilment he was capable of, that was still *hoping* that he would. Everyone else just had themselves to think about but I had me and the unknown quantity that is Sherlock to get all brushed-up. It was a best-bib-and-tucker day so we all wanted to look our best. Sherlock was going to be in his uniform of his red-and-black harness, and I wondered if he should wear his red-and-black boots too, since it could be a conversation point. My dress uniform didn't need too much dusting off because of all the outreach work Sherlock and I do representing the Fire Dogs. Most of those events require the more formal attire, so at least I knew my uniform still fitted me and that all I needed to do was shine up the buttons!

Soon it was time to line up, and I was standing at the end of the fire crew with Sherlock in my arms. Better to keep him close to me like that, where I could see what he was up to. I didn't want Wonder Dog to miss out just because he was at my feet the whole time, and I gathered that the royal party would probably prefer him to be within easy reach too. My eyes were fixed on the royal party making its way down the line. The wait was agonising, as I hoped that Sherlock would sit still for just a while longer. As His Royal Highness got closer, I claimed a firmer grip on Sherlock, but not too firm in case he started back-peddling to get down. I was talking to him, nice and calm: 'You good boy, you're such a good boy, Rockster ... Now, you're going to be the best dog ever ... That's it ... Good lad ...' all the time trying to make up for the fact that he didn't have his ball to chew. No ball – no slobber. That was the idea. But like a dummy-dependent toddler, Sherlock was wondering: If I don't have the ball, and Dad doesn't have the ball – then who's got my ball?

Before long, it was our turn and His Royal Highness was with us, focusing immediately on Sherlock. Prince Charles stayed with us a good two or three minutes, asking about Sherlock's role and the impact the Fire Dogs have on an investigation, and discussing how they help to catch the people responsible and ultimately contribute to making our city safer.

As I was talking, Sherlock was looking for something. He was distracted. Where was that ball? In a very brave move, my daring dog leant over and licked the royal hand! Maybe he thought Prince Charles was the one hiding the ball all this time. Thankfully, His Royal Highness didn't flinch, but gave him a warm smile – Sherlock really does charm everyone! Apart from that slightly nerve wracking moment, the day passed without incident.

That day was the highlight of a very special year for the Brigade, and for me and Sherlock too. Suddenly, the press was on our tail and it was wonderful to see the focus on the men and women on the front line, and other less well-known units, like the Fire Investigation Team, getting some recognition too. I guess it's easy for the public to see something every day and still not notice that it's there – even if it is a twelve-tonne fire engine painted bright red. There seems to be very little respite from the sound of one or another of the Emergency Services' vehicles working their way through the capital to reach someone in need. We are always aware of the sirens even when we are not in uniform, and we can't help wondering who is going where and why, but we appreciate that to the public the blues and twos are just part of the general city noise – the London buzz – and that perhaps they have become a little desensitised.

The 150th anniversary celebrations gave the Brigade an opportunity to remind people what the Brigade is all about and the important role it plays in our society. Before the London Fire Brigade was formed in 1866 there was very little in the way of fire-prevention awareness and fire safety, and, because each borough was responsible for its own emergency service, there was sometimes nothing more than a blanket and a bucket of water between you and your house burning to the ground.

Throughout the year, the crews visited at least 150 schools to talk about the London Fire Brigade, our history and our work today. As I mentioned before school visits are something we do regularly, and we have an education wing that looks after that for us, but the anniversary was a chance to talk about how the Brigade came into existence and the impact of two great historical events on its expansion: the Great Fire of London in 1666, and what became known as the Second Great Fire of London which took place on the night of 29 December 1940, when around 100,000 bombs were dropped on to the capital by the German Luftwaffe, causing a blaze so ferocious it destroyed the Square Mile of the City and claimed the lives of fourteen firefighters. Children love it when you bring history alive, and we're lucky to have such a rich history to share. The impact of these stories on the children is amazing to see. It's putting the Brigade into context and showing how we have been there, playing our part, during some of the most pivotal moments in British history.

As I've said, as a boy I always thought I would have a career in the RAF and would follow in the footsteps of my grandfathers who enjoyed their time in the military, so finding myself doing talks about our wartime Prime Minister Winston Churchill and his instruction, on the evening of 29 December 1940, to the then Deputy Chief Officer, Major Frank W. Jackson, to 'save the cathedral at all costs' always blows me away! And we had our own firefighter heroes from the night to inspire the children, including Jack Corbett, who answered that call out from Churchill as a volunteer, and risked his life in the process. Jack was 105 years old when he died in his sleep in 2016, just days after receiving his own copy of the Brigade's anniversary book at a special ceremony at his home in Essex. Jack would have seen people's lives taken, their homes destroyed, and all he could do was his best to protect them, just as we do today. But it was the action of the Fire Brigade and Auxiliary Fire Brigade volunteers like Jack that changed how the Service was seen forever after by the public. After their actions during the Second Great Fire of London they came to be known as the 'heroes with grimy faces'.

What I find really important to share with the children is how things changed so much, and for the better, after the Second World War. Today the London Fire Brigade operates out of 103 fire stations. It is the busiest fire-and-rescue service in the country, and is one of the largest firefighting and rescue organisations in the world. Operators at the Brigade's call centre handle around 500 calls a day from members of the public to attend a variety of incidents, including house and commercial property fires, road traffic accidents, people getting trapped in something, or locked out of something and there will always be the hoax calls. And sadly, it's not a joke that people will call the Fire Brigade to rescue their cat from up a tree, or if their sink gets blocked, or they've lost their keys, wasting thousands of pounds in public money.

During the celebrations, I was really honoured to be presented with a Borough Commander's Letter of Congratulations (a bit like a military Mention in Dispatches) for unfaltering work on behalf of the Brigade. It was all off-duty work, and not done for the overtime pay but because we knew the dogs' visits would mean a lot to a great many people. It's good to be recognised, but since we love the job, everyone wins.

The anniversary also saw Sherlock immortalised for his work for the Brigade in a special celebration edition of Monopoly. The famous board game, all about buying property in London, is a family favourite and everyone has their favourite counter. Arguments have raged over who gets what out of the eight on offer, and changes made to the line-up over the years have sparked a few harsh words too, but the Scottie dog, added in the 1950s, has always been popular. But in the London Fire Brigade 150th Anniversary Special Edition the dog counter is based on … Sherlock!

I was so chuffed when they told me. Just think, he will be part of that version forever! I'm sure it was Sherlock's first real brush with stardom. Meeting with the people from Hasbro, who produce Monopoly, was really exciting and Sherlock was very happy having his photograph taken – which was a relief. I think, like me, he was a bit shocked and surprised, but it didn't matter; we had a great day, and some months later when we saw the little Sherlock counters it was amazing. Sherlock didn't look overly impressed, but my colleagues and family were happy and proud, and who wouldn't be? It's another way to celebrate the anniversary, and, since Sherlock is a name so synonymous with London, you never know – the public could vote for him to move into the mainstream game!

Not long after the Fire Brigade celebrated their anniversary, I marked one of my own: twenty years in the Fire Service. When I was told that I would be presented with my twenty-year Long Service and Good Conduct Medal with my family beside me I was over the moon. Believe me, you don't do this job on your own – your family joins the Brigade too! It was to be presented by Commissioner Dany Cotton in September 2017, but there was one disappointment – Sherlock wasn't allowed into City Hall (the Mayor of London's office) where the ceremony would take place. I was upset about that and I knew the Commissioner would be disappointed too, as she is Sherlock's number-one fan and, when you think about it, in dog years he has racked up thirty-five years' service for the Brigade!

Never mind, rules are rules and I told him that he could see all the photos after the event, which was wonderful. Kate, Olivia, Emma, Mum and Dad were there mingling with the Brigade's top brass. Charlie, my boss, met my family, which was very special for me. And the girls were delighted for me – and were happy because they were given permission to have the day off school to attend and have a celebration meal at Jamie Oliver's restaurant afterwards.

In that one day twenty years' worth of hard work, great memories, countless friends and lots of fun came into focus. My dad was right: 'Do what you believe in and follow your dreams' and 'Just try your hardest.' They will always be the strongest words he's said to me and now I say the same to my girls. I don't want them to be pressured into being top of the class or the best at everything, because that can be a recipe for disaster. Pushing someone in any direction is unlikely to work. I want happy, healthy, confident children who know that trying your best will make you happier than being on a pedestal where others can push you off. They know Kate and I are happy as long as they try. Winning a race isn't essential to winning a tournament. I've been last loads of times, learnt lessons and tried again – slow and steady wins the race!

Chapter 20

And the Winner is …

In a year that was all about celebrating the heritage of the London Fire Brigade, it was no surprise that I could hear Mick's words ringing in my mind: 'Our job is all about keeping people safe and that is what we do.' It was so wonderful to see Mick and his Springer Spaniel, Roscoe, honoured at the 2016 Animal Hero Awards presented by the charity the International Fund for Animal Welfare (IFAW), because, having spent thirty years with the Service, and thirteen of those as an investigator and dog handler before his retirement in 2017, Mick deserved this as much as Roscoe did. Roscoe was awarded the title Animal of the Year for his work as a Fire Investigation Dog, and Mick proudly collected the award, with Roscoe at his side, at a special ceremony at the House of Lords, surrounded by celebrities, charity bosses and politicians. It was an event that showcased the work of the Fire Dog like never before.

What a great thing to happen in the Brigade's 150th anniversary year. Mick and Roscoe winning that award put the story of the Fire Dogs out there and recognised a job that Roscoe had been carrying out for thirteen years. This was an award we could all be proud of and, at the same time, we were all very happy for Mick. If I remember rightly, he had to get a few rounds in on the back of that one!

Working with Fire Investigation Dogs like Sherlock is incredibly rewarding, but I don't think any of us expected to start bringing actual silverware home for it! When Roscoe was named Animal of the Year by the IFAW in 2016 it marked the start of a flurry of accolades to honour the London Fire Brigade's dogs. Then the National Office of Animal Health (NOAH) presented their Contribution to Society Award to Murphy and Mick, and it really felt as though it was time for the dogs to shine and for Mick's hard work to be fully recognised outside the Brigade. This was confirmed again when the Worshipful Company of Security Professionals presented the Dog Team with their award for 'outstanding service in the protection of people, property and liberty'. The outside world was watching, and loving what they saw. Understanding of dogs' skill and devotion to duty was out there – at last.

When the London Fire Brigade's Fire Investigation Dogs were declared winners in the *Daily Mirror* and RSPCA Animal Hero Awards 2017 we all felt so proud of our four-legged workmates. We already felt they were heroes, our very own heroes, but to have such public recognition for their work was quite something. This was it.

The award recognised our dogs, Roscoe, Murphy and Sherlock, who, the award's board said 'exemplified the heroism of Britain's public-service animals'. It was the proudest moment for me and Sherlock and for Mick with Roscoe and Murphy. The year 2017 witnessed a string of horrific events: terror attacks in London and Manchester and the seventy-two lives lost in the Grenfell Tower fire moved the country to tears. The remarkable courage, dedication and selflessness of our Emergency Services inspired the nation, and Service dogs would have been present in some capacity in each instance. The Brigade's Fire Investigation Dogs were praised for their dedication when attending around 200 fires a year and for their skill in determining the cause.

At the time of the award ceremony Mick Boyle had only just retired. His dogs, Murphy and Roscoe, were honoured on the night, but it felt as though it should also have been a lifetime achievement award for Mick, who said:

The dogs are all about keeping the people of London safe and they have been an exceptional success. Every time I work with them and they find something it gives me immense satisfaction and I'm always amazed. I never ever get tired of it when they do find something. I've always had pride in my two dogs.

The awards' organisers were keen to have as many dogs as possible at the event with their handlers, but Mick and I were of the same opinion: our dogs plus a three-course meal in the Grosvenor Hotel in London (plus alcohol) don't mix! Add to that a number of other dogs that ours could disagree with and that would be enough to destroy the organisers' idea of a line-up of obedient Fire Dogs sitting patiently at our feet while everyone enjoyed the ceremony.

A plan was hatched with one of my team, Matt, who agreed to bring all three dogs to the venue close to the time the award was to be presented. We had been given the exact time of the presentation so that made life a bit easier, and Matt was happy to oblige. The only issue was that we forgot to share with him how grumpy Sherlock can be with Roscoe and Murphy. Let's say they don't always see eye to eye (to eye!).

Totally unaware of any potential problem, Matt headed to the Grosvenor where he ran headlong into the wonderful

Paul O'Grady who, because of his huge love of dogs, couldn't resist getting up close and personal with our little band of brothers. Sadly for Matt, Roscoe decided to choose that moment to mount an all-teeth-showing attack on Sherlock, who was having none of it and gave Roscoe a piece of his mind. While Sherlock was giving it some verbal and Roscoe was going all hair and teeth, Matt put his leg in between them and got his knee bitten! Unsurprisingly, Paul sensibly decided to make a quick exit, giving London's finest a wide berth!

Trying not to show any pain or embarrassment, Matt caught up with us and told his tale. I hope he wasn't expecting any sympathy because he didn't get any – we were too busy laughing at his expense! We hoped that he would forgive us if he got to stay for a while after the presentation, and it seemed only fair since he had agreed to take the dogs back with him when it was all over.

Stepping up for the award was quite something. Although we knew in advance what we were getting, it was still quite a moment hearing our names read out and a description of the dogs' achievements. It was almost as if it was happening to someone else. Like an out-of-body experience. And then suddenly we found ourselves walking towards the stage where Richard Hammond of *Top Gear* fame was waiting to make the presentation. He's a great animal lover, and of course his own occupational hazards have put him in touch with the Emergency Services a few times over recent years. Richard was a great choice to present the award because you could tell that he had a real feeling for and appreciation of our work. Our moment on stage only lasted seconds but the wave of applause that came over us from the audience is something that I will remember for years.

Immediately after the ceremony we went off for a press photo call and we were in demand for interviews too. It was very exciting, and I was so happy that the dogs were getting the recognition they deserved. Mick and I wanted to make sure that we did our best by them. By the time we had finished that first round we were too excited, and when it was time to rejoin the audience we decided that we would stand at the back of the room rather than return to our table. It was better for the dogs too because they were just as excited as we were!

Ironically, instead of getting the space and peace we wanted for the dogs we started to attract a new audience! Once people noticed where we were they started coming over to take photographs and talk to us about our newly crowned hero dogs. Mick and I chatted with people for the best part of a couple of hours, which must have been a bit of a pain for Kate and Mick's wife, Sue. But they are used to us abandoning them at events where the dogs are the centre of attention. I know Kate loves to see me and Sherlock get mobbed by so many interested folk, but it happens wherever we go, and I appreciate that it can get a bit repetitive! The same happens wherever we go as a team and on open days; it's nothing for us to be answering questions for three to four hours. People want to know the same things: what does your dog do? How old is he? What's his name? How long did it take to train him? Why does he wear boots? By the time you've finished with the last question you usually have other folk pushing in asking the first question again! But it's wonderful really because very often people have never heard of a Fire Investigation Dog, and by the time we've finished talking they are new fans. And Sherlock never gets bored of being on interview duty – as long as he has his ball!

Suffice it to say, the dogs went down really well with the audience at the Grosvenor that night. There were several celebrities attending but I really wasn't on the ball so didn't think to get photographs with anyone. It would have been great for us have pictures, and good for PR and for social media. It sounds obvious in hindsight but to be honest I was so overwhelmed by the whole event that I just went with the flow!

I would say that evening was one of the highlights of my career so far. That and meeting Prince Charles. It was the night where I had all my suspicions confirmed – that people love these dogs and genuinely want to know more about them.

While I was taking Sherlock for a leg-stretch during the ceremony, Angela Rippon, the ex-television newsreader and now presenter of consumer programmes, tracked me down. She said that she had been looking for me – and more importantly for Sherlock! She had met him as a puppy when Dave first had him and she had followed his progress. She added that she had voted for us to win the Animal Hero Award because of all the invaluable work we do to protect the people of London. It was very humbling to have such a hugely respected celebrity broadcaster think of us in that way. She reminded me that the public had voted for this award and that that was an important point. This wasn't an in-house accolade, or something corporate, this was recognition from the public – which clearly included celebrities too – and that meant everything to me for Sherlock and the team, and all those handlers and dogs who had gone before us, as well as the other thirteen teams working around the country.

If it was a surprise to be approached by Angela Rippon, it was even more surreal sharing a few jokes with my new friend Richard Hammond, since the closest I had been to him before that night was watching him on the telly in *Top*

Gear and *The Grand Tour*. Truth be told, I didn't get long enough to actually talk to him earlier in the evening, so as he was leaving at the end of the night I introduced myself – apologising to his wife for holding him up – and asked for a quick photo with him so I had something to show my friends and a memory of a special night … otherwise I might not have believed it myself come the morning. His wife was very gracious, and Richard was very kind – just as you see him on screen. I don't get to mingle with the stars every day, so I was a little star-struck to say the least.

It was a night full of celebrities and although we didn't get to meet a great many of them because there was so much going on, everyone wanted to speak to *us*, so we had more than our fifteen minutes of fame. It was very strange! But being recognised isn't about me at all – it's always all about Sherlock. Mick said to me, even before I got the job, that the role is all about the dogs because they don't really need us! The human value in the relationship is the ability to accurately interpret the dogs' behaviour while they are working. Sherlock's body language is where all the answers lie. He does his job and I guide and interpret. Together we come up with the goods. Without the dog's skills the job would not exist. It's only ever about my clever, loyal sidekick – my boy. He deserves the recognition, because with him on the team we have a game-changer, and as a team we can go anywhere, do anything and catch anyone. He's the one who makes me look good!

Watching our dogs receive their Animal Hero Award, they looked like three incredible creatures, and anyone who thought that was absolutely right. Seeing them standing at the feet of Mick and me in uniform would have made it clear that these were working dogs. The breeds – a Springer Spaniel, and two Cocker Spaniels – might have been a bit of a giveaway, since they are intelligent, inquisitive and driven by nature. Roscoe, Murphy and Sherlock all show the best in their breed. They are not just great dogs, they are extraordinary dogs. And now Sherlock is continuing with the incredible training devised by Clive to ensure that he is working at his highest level.

The dogs have brought each other on and Sherlock as the baby in the trio has benefited from having the older, wiser guys at his side. It is not common for dogs to work a search area together, but it can happen if the search covers one or two days and there is an overlap of shifts; also, in training having a second keen nose on the job can work well.

Mick and I have only overlapped on searches where one of ours has searched before the scene has been excavated and then the other has gone in after. Rerunning the dogs over the scene has provided useful confirmation. It often helps explain their behaviours, as in the case of the fire in the thatched cottage, where Sherlock indicated on a spot beneath the overhang of the thatch and then Mick, with Murphy and Roscoe, went in the following day and found fuel containers exactly where Sherlock had indicated the day before. We often worked together in training with Clive and that's where, by observing our dogs' behaviour, we learnt really valuable lessons which would prove very useful in operational searches. To have a second dog educates us as handlers because we can view how the two dogs act differently in training and then translate that into nurturing their skills, so they can be operationally more competent.

The Fire Investigation Dogs receive the best of training to enable them to do the best possible job. Regular training keeps them working at the highest level possible. However, it takes thousands of pounds to train and maintain each dog – if you have a dog of your own you'll know what I mean! And this is not government funded, so money has to be found from hard-pressed existing budgets and supplemented through fundraising events and community campaigns. Considering the amazing work these guys do, it's a good investment, and certainly the London Fire Brigade is reaping the benefits. The London model works well, and Sherlock, as the lone dog at the moment, is flying the flag – and wagging his tail – for Fire Dogs.

The year 2017 will be remembered as a challenging one for the Emergency Services. It was a year that tested everything we have to offer, and I believe that we passed the test – with flying colours. But the echo and ripple effect of everything that happened in London and Manchester will not go away, and there are certainly still lessons to learn. Commemorating the thirtieth anniversary of the King's Cross fire was a sobering experience. We still have serving officers who were in attendance that night and the memories of that do not leave you – ever. Lives were lost that evening and lessons are still being learnt. But we are always learning, as are the dogs. We will always look for new ways to extend their skills and we know the dogs will respond, eager to work for us and play their game. There's probably no limit to what we can do with the dogs and what they can do for us. It's possible that we have really only just begun.

I look at Sherlock sitting beside me, a deconstructed tennis ball beside him. He takes the newly stripped ball into his mouth and chews it for comfort. He's happy. The ball is another Sherlock-shredded victim with its hairy green exterior nibbled and sucked to a slimy pulp that he has set to one side. 'Well, that's a lovely mess you've made of that if I may say so, Sherlock! Good job I've got a few more of those in store because I'll bet that will be a mass of chewed-up rubber the next time I look!'

Award-winning dog, eh? You bet!

Chapter 21

The Best Job in the World

Thinking about it, Sherlock has never really known how significant he and his other Fire Investigation Dog colleagues across the country are, but his drive and skills are serving the British people well day in, day out. His training followed that of Star, Sam, Roscoe and Murphy before him, and he has enjoyed everything about the positive-reinforcement-based training programme, which, as Sherlock well knows, ends in that tennis ball being offered to him as a reward for detecting an ignitable substance. To keep his senses sharp he is regularly tested on a number of disciplines and in a number of environments, including a single room, several rooms on different floors, and test areas such as letter boxes and under stairs. As new challenges arise for the firefighters and investigators, so the dogs are trained to detect in new areas for substances that are new to them. As the threats and deeds of the arsonist extend, so must the work of the Fire Investigation Dogs. It's never easy to stay one step ahead of the 'enemy', but we have to at least keep pace with them.

Arson is, as we've seen, the crime the Fire Investigation Dog is looking to help prove or disprove. It's a huge threat to any community or individual, and just under a third of all fires attended by the London Fire Brigade are started deliberately.[1] Sometimes it's youngsters lighting a fire because they're bored or curious, but sometimes the reasons can be financial or a cry for help. One thing is for sure: if there's an accelerant to blame, Sherlock will find it, and that 'find' could contribute to the conviction of the arsonist. If the fire has resulted in a death Sherlock's evidence could be crucial in a murder case, especially if he detects anything that could incriminate the arsonist – if, for example, they have left their DNA on discarded clothes, petrol rags or protective gloves. The power of the dog's nose could make all the difference.

Crime scenes are growing more complex as rival gangs and terrorists increase their threats and the nature of their

---

[1] 'Fire Facts: Fires in Greater London 1966–2016', London Fire Brigade, December 2017.

'businesses' grows more violent. When the gangs' calling card is petrol on a doormat followed by a lit match, then you know what you are up against, but you also know that if that's today's threat then there is likely to be a worse act to follow. This is where working with the police and forensic professionals is so important, as is mutual trust and appreciation.

There are around 4,500 firefighters in the London Fire Brigade and at present only one dog: Sherlock. At one time the dog would have been an untested novelty at a crime scene, and no doubt the butt of a few jokes. I'm sure Clive had to get used to jibes and the usual 'What's your dog do, mate?' The pressure was on to prove something, and, from the other side, the pressure was put on to find something. As soon as your dog is put under pressure to do anything he will want to find something just to please you, and that's not a great position to be in. But things have changed.

Now the dog handler is in charge because the handler will not put his dog in an unsafe position. He will also trust his dog to find something if it's there – or nothing if the scene is clear. There's no pressure, only respect from everyone present for what the dog can do. Everyone cares about the dog.

Only last year I was asked to take Sherlock to a fire scene in an area where their Brigade had recently been forced, by costs, to let its Fire Investigation Dog Team go. They had two cases, and both had the look of arson about them. They knew a dog would be able to tell them everything that they needed to know, so Sherlock and I were called in. In less than fifteen minutes he had searched and indicated, giving the police officers present something to shape their investigation. For me it was sad that this Fire and Rescue Service no longer had their own dog, due to financial constraints. Being used to having a canine detective they knew only a dog could help them in the case. It was good they had Sherlock to call on and we were happy to help.

Recognition is the greatest step forward the dogs have made. In the beginning there was disbelief that a dog could add anything to the party, but in just over twenty years the attitude has changed to: can we please have a dog to get this party started? I like showing Sherlock off because I'm proud of what he can achieve in the work we do. Changing attitudes and getting serious about Fire Dogs is one of my crusades.

One day early on in my time as a dog handler, the dog van broke down in Braintree in Essex and I was stuck calling for help to tow the van away and get me and Sherlock back to Dowgate. The recovery vehicle responsible for recovering the dog van arrived – and I was totally shocked to hear that the recovery vechicle didn't accomodate dogs!

'But you're recovering the Fire Dog Team! In that case, mate, we'll be travelling up front with you!' With that I collected Sherlock in my arms and we sat in the front passenger seat with him connected to me in his harness. He loved it! He never has a view of where he is going from his kennel in the back of the dog van, so he was revelling in the wind in his hair, a view and new smells. I could almost see it on his face: 'Look, Dad, great view from here. Look at that! And that!' His head was swirling around. I wasn't glad that the van had broken down, but it was worth it to see the sheer joy on Sherlock's face!

I'm sure that situation wouldn't happen now. The Fire Investigation Dogs are more high-profile and everyone within the Service knows that wherever I go Sherlock will be with me. We come as a package of Fire Investigator and Investigation Dog, which is actually quite unusual because sometimes the handler is not an investigator. The role of the dogs and their remit is still something that is filtering through the system, but the best way for that to quicken up is for people to see Sherlock in action. Whenever I get the chance and my colleagues are able to spare the time I show them Sherlock in action. It's just a matter of placing something in the yard for him to find, but the look of incredulity on their faces always pleases me. You can tell that, at first, they are wondering what the dog can do – maybe if he can do anything at all – but then comes the moment when Sherlock hits on the hidden substance. And it's a showstopper!

I can hear them saying: 'He's done it! Look, he's found it! How did he do that? That's amazing!' I love hearing that. It really makes my day because I'm so proud of him and I naturally want others to see him and feel that same buzz.

Working with the police I've seen an increased appreciation of the dogs' skills on a search too. I'm very proud to be the handler of a dog who can deliver results in a matter of minutes. Results that would take days for human beings to collate and, even then, they would not have the accuracy of a dog's nose. I'm proud of Sherlock, and I know the whole team are too.

It's not just us though – everyone has worked hard for this feedback from third parties. It's thanks to Clive and then Dave and Mick that the Brigade is now reaping the benefits of the Fire Investigation Dogs. I recall Clive telling me that when he first worked Star the greatest sceptics were the forensic teams. He tells the tale of a forensic guy who wouldn't wait for the Fire Dog to arrive, so he went ahead on the evidence he could see, which led him to put the fire down to an electrical accident. But when the dog came on the scene it hit on accelerant in the room almost immediately. The forensic guy was so impressed with the dog's speed and accuracy that on his next case he asked for a dog to search before anything was touched. It was the right decision because the dog picked up the scent of ignitable fluids right away. Clive had a convert and that was an important milestone in the journey of the dogs that he had championed. If there was ever a sector whose endorsement would give the dogs credibility, it was the forensic department – and there it was.

To have the scientists believe in the dogs' skills and abilities was a massive step forward. It was proof that all the training and dedication was no longer an experiment or a whim – it was real, and that was enough to give Clive ammunition to throw at any detractors and push his case for the future of Hydrocarbon Detection Dogs in the Brigade.

The dogs have had to prove their worth all along. There hasn't been any let-up or favours flung their way, so each handler knows that when their dogs have passed their graduation and Certification they really have made the grade on their own merit. Year upon year they have blasted everyone away with their work ethic and accuracy. That Mick Boyle saw the dogs progress to the point where Roscoe was named Animal of the Year by the International Fund for Animal Welfare (IFAW) in 2016 was an incredible achievement – for him and all of us. What that award said to everyone else, to me and Sherlock included, was

… we've made it! To have the team honoured with the Animal Hero Award by the *Daily Mirror* and the RSPCA in 2017 truly put the icing on the top of the cake!

When I got my dream job, and what turned out to be my dream dog, in 2013, I remember feeling very, very proud for two reasons: firstly because I got the job at all, and secondly because that job gave me a place on one of the most elite teams in the London Fire Brigade and in one of the most specialist groups in the country. As Clive had always said to me, the dogs are a special tool in the box and we must always remember that. Now it appeared that others were seeing the dogs in those special terms too. But to achieve that level of recognition everyone had pulled together to translate hard work into exceptional success. When Roscoe and Murphy retired with Mick in August 2017, those two dogs had attended more than 2,000 incidents. Sherlock is out on operations at least three to four times a week, and in his first year with me he had sniffed out enough evidence to contribute to ten separate convictions. I can't help wondering if the convictions would have been possible without Sherlock's expertise on those searches. Sherlock, the 'special tool in the box' with the incredibly sensitive nose is a little crimebuster all on his own. It makes you wonder how we managed without these amazing Fire Dogs and how other Brigades have to manage without one. They are excellent value for money and you certainly get a return on your investment. Without Sherlock's skills, how many guilty people would simply walk free? The dogs are a living, breathing, working asset, and are so much better and more reliable than the techno Gastec – which is now kept mostly in the cupboard! There is nothing better than Sherlock's nose for getting the job done and nothing better for our work discipline. The dogs win hands down every time.

Saying that, Sherlock may not be flying solo for much longer – soon there might be a canine Watson to join the team if he makes it through the tough selection processes. Although he's a long way from graduation yet, a new dog – a Springer Spaniel called Simba – alongside his handler Anton, are currently in training. It's still early days but the signs are looking good, and everyone at the Brigade has got their fingers crossed that Simba will show the same instinctive drive – and love for tennis balls – that our investigation dogs need.

Sherlock's job in the Brigade is more than 'detective'; he's a learning aid and confidence builder and general all-round friend to everyone. He's one of the good guys and you know where you are with Sherlock – he just gets on with the job and loves every minute of it. Dogs are honest – it's all they know, and that's good in Sherlock's job because it's the kind of absolute clarity needed to perform accurately. If he indicates on a scent, then he has found something. There is no need for second-guessing and no room for doubt. Sherlock is likely the most reliable member of staff on the books – and the least likely to ask for a pay rise!

In my twenty years with the Brigade I have seen changes and advances in many areas. I joined as a firefighter to make a positive difference to people's lives but realised early on in my career that identifying causes of fire and trying to reduce or eliminate them is more positive than seeing someone's lifelong possessions disappear never to be replaced. Sometimes what is achieved away from incidents, using information gathered and opening up dialogue between different organisations, can be really valuable in making people's lives, houses and workplaces safer. A good example of this interaction, involving the London Fire Brigade, appliance manufacturers and Members of Parliament, is the Total Recalls campaign (www.london-fire.gov.uk/product-recalls.asp). The Fire Investigation Team has added real momentum to this campaign to bring about positive change and make good on our promise of 'making London a safer city' – it's not just a collection of words but a fact. I am proud to have been one of the team achieving this, and I'm proud that my dog Sherlock has been by my side the whole time.

For me, this is what the job is all about: effecting change for the better. We don't just put out fires, we investigate fires, find out why they happen, and work with the appropriate body or organisation to ensure that further fires can be prevented. Ultimately, in an ideal world, the Fire Brigade doesn't want there to be fires to fight. Protecting the public from situations that cause fires and people who set fires is where we want to be. And this is where skilled dogs like Sherlock come in, playing their part in protecting members of a community and getting to the truth at the source of a fire so the appropriate action can be taken.

Taking fire investigation to the next level is bound to involve discussions with Parliament at some point. In 2017 I had the honour of being asked to present to the parliamentary working group for animal welfare – the All-party Parliamentary Dog Advisory Welfare Group (APDAWG) – which also covers the Unsung Heroes: Dogs That Help, Support & Protect Our Society. This was the greatest opportunity to promote the work of the Brigade's Fire Investigation Team and our dogs. I saw this as a chance to show MPs, and the movers and shakers in the world of animal welfare, the real value of what we achieve.

The Brigade is often at parliament in some capacity or other, we have a presence there, but most of the time we are in the back door and out again without the press or anyone really knowing what we have achieved. However; I'm pleased to share that we were very well received and attracted quite a crowd at the end of the presentation. People wanted to know more about our work and what we are trying to achieve with the dogs and through our investigation work. I'm equally pleased to say that my PR wingman aka Sherlock was being his usual handsome self and was very obliging when asked to have his photograph taken wearing his special protective boots. He's used to it now – the novelty dog wearing boots is a well-seasoned role for the furry lover of the spotlight and it catches people's attention with the cute factor, which is often all that's needed to get us over the threshold to engage with our audience.

During our visit to Parliament we were met by Sir David Amess MP, whose work on the advisory group for fire safety has been very supportive of our investigation team. It was very special receiving a thank-you letter from an MP wishing my family a happy Christmas. Something about it had a feel of promise and hope for our work. There is now an additional opportunity to present to the fire safety parliamentary working group, and who knows where that could lead? Times, I feel, are a-changing for the better. There is a massively positive feel to everything we are doing and trying to achieve for our dogs in the future. And all the time Sherlock is alongside me, but now people don't need to ask: 'What does your dog do?' because the dogs' achievements are out there, opening doors and inviting people to sit up and take notice of their worth.

In the end, however, although we've been running around to the Houses of Parliament to attract attention and support, we still have our community to serve and protect. Community is our priority because that is where we can directly achieve the most results in education, fire awareness, and can broadcast to the criminal fraternity that the investigation team is here to catch you. Detective Sherlock has the capability to detect evidence that can secure a conviction. That is a capability that the Brigade couldn't offer to the police and CPS before 2000 – but it's there now.

Chapter 22

A Dog Like No Other

A fter a long day when Sherlock's having one of his quieter moments, sitting chewing or lying spark-out in his kennel, I go and sit alongside him for a chat. He can be still, I promise you that it is possible – it's just that he doesn't do it very often. Even when he is relaxing, his large, twinkly, soft brown eyes, lashing tail and swaggering body movements are only ever just a millisecond from bursting into action and bringing a smile to my face – and to anyone else's who's watching him too. The whole package that is Sherlock is so infectious.

'You OK there, Sherlock? What have you found to chew?' I ask him, but I can see that it's one of his Christmas squeaky toys that's been rediscovered after a bit of tasty weathering in the garden. 'Now you be careful with that and try not to shred it beyond all recognition. Although now you have it on the go I'm sure I won't see it looking like a snowman for much longer!' Sherlock loves his toys, but he can be guilty of loving them too much and that's when they start to do a disappearing act – sometimes bit by bit.

I hope Sherlock isn't lonely in his little world of work, toys and home with us. He never seems to be and, as long as he has a ball, he never barks – unless he wants to really make his presence felt when there is another dog around. He strikes me as a bit of a loner who chooses his own company when and if he needs it. He makes the best of his downtime with a bit of Sherlock-time and I don't think there is anything wrong with that.

If Kate is ever asked about Sherlock she will always say that to understand Sherlock someone needs to know me too, because in her eyes we are not just dog and handler, we are made of the same stuff. 'They are both always busy and never still!' is her take on things.

Paul 'rests' by keeping busy in the garden, completing some DIY in the house or launching into a torturous exercise routine … That's if he's not on the school run or working through a to-do list at blistering speed. It's how he is, how he has always been, and there is a similar 'let's reach the stars right now' streak in Sherlock too.

The first time I met Sherlock I thought his backside had to be on batteries because it never stops moving. It goes from side to side no matter what he is up to. And his tail is like a crazy rudder fighting to keep him on four paws. Looking at him from the rear he looks like an out-of-control bumper car! It really is the funniest thing.

I never expected a working dog to be affectionate. Like Paul, I grew up with dogs, so I had an idea of what we were inviting into our home, but I didn't count on Sherlock being Sherlock! Destructive in the garden and bit of a thief in the house, he's not what most people would think of as pet material because he has such a high work drive, but, when he's feeling tired, or a bit below par, he will snuggle up for some affection. It's Sherlock's way of letting us know that he wants to be close to us as much as we want to be close to him. It's lovely really, and I see the girls respond with all the cuddles in the world. That's family for you – and Sherlock is family.

Just recently the Rockster had a run-in with a dog in the local park. It was a new dog on the patch and was probably trying to flex his muscles a bit so picked on the fluffy spaniel as an easy target. Sherlock didn't take the beating lying down but he did come away limping, which wasn't good to see. That was the end of walktime for that night, and I have to say that he looked happy to be home and headed for his favourite spot in the kitchen. For once Sherlock looked as if he could do with a big hug and the girls were on to that right away. We still had to make a trip to see the vet, but it was the dog's reaction to cuddles from Olivia and Emma that was so touching. He lay in their arms and took every bit of love and affection they had to offer – and that was a lot!

It wasn't long before Sherlock was back on his feet, albeit still with a faint limp. It's not easy to stick to the vet's advice of 'lots of rest' when you have a driven power pack for a dog. As you can imagine, being kept on a short lead is far from his idea of heaven. No one who wants to just run free, like Sherlock, likes the feel of a collar and leash pulling them back. He was not a happy bunny. It's also funny for me to have him virtually tied to me because I'm not used to that. I like to see Sherlock running with the wind in his hair and the sun on his back. He is a true free spirit and not so much a work dog as a spaniel in full flight! But that's when he goes looking for trouble and almost always finds it!

'Hey, Sherlock, do you remember when you dug that hole and covered the back of that person's coat with mud?

'Do you remember when you dived behind the garden trampoline to hide from the wheelbarrow?

'Do you remember when you carved out a crater when we were on a Sunday-morning walk with the girls and you covered the two of them in clods of earth? They do!'

It's funny and he is funny; even though in many ways Sherlock is all about the job and puts his whole being into every search, he is still a crazy dog.

I watch his body language very closely during a search and I see that every fibre, every sinew of his body is focused on what he is doing. His concentration is second to none and that's how he works his way over an area so quickly and efficiently – his nose down and his bum in the air, swaying so much from side to side that it looks like his bum will run alongside his head. I can't help smiling as I watch him but there is another part of me that has to admire him. Sherlock is a star – no doubt about that.

We work long hours and we see lots of things we wouldn't want others to. I try to maintain the balance between what I must do and what is important for my own mental health.

I'm often asked about the time I spent in Aldgate Station during the 7/7 bombings and I can say that at the time I was doing what was required of me as a firefighter, but the lasting pain came from the fact that my hands were tied – I couldn't save all the lives that time. I was helpless. And it gave me nightmares, which returned when I had to relive that day in court. It unlocked a memory that I thought I had successfully transferred to a place I knew it would be safe and laid peacefully to rest in a deep recess of my brain. I don't know if I will ever be free of those memories.

As a Fire Investigator and Sherlock's handler I *don't* feel helpless. I know that with Sherlock we are going to have positive results at the end of the day – even in the worst of cases: a fatality. There can't be anything worse. But Sherlock and I can find answers, which may provide closure. More than that, in this job we can protect and reach out. And who is the best of all communicators? Sherlock, of course!

This role requires commitment and I'm lucky that I am the kind of person who not only needs to identify a problem but who won't give up until he has provided a number of solutions. The thing is, the commitment must come from everyone around you and I'm so lucky that my family is always there to support me when I'm on my highs but also when I sometimes hit a low – and that usually happens when there has been no closure in a case. My family knows that they have me 100 per cent, but sometimes I will be dealing with someone else's loved one until well past the end of my shift. And sometimes Sherlock will be the one who gets tucked up in bed last because he needed to run off the day as much as me.

Kate says:

Wherever they are together, I know they are looking after each other. I feel that now we have Sherlock I have two versions of Paul – both crazy, both full of energy – and Olivia and Emma have a daddy and his naughty friend. Man and dog are both determined to do their job to the best of their ability and love us with all their hearts. For that they both have our deep love and huge respect. I'd just love to see them stand still for a moment so the rest of us can catch up!

When I started the job, people spoke of a learning curve: it's not a curve – it's an educational Mount Everest! I have never worked harder in my career, but I have never been happier in my work, for standing by my side is Sherlock ... the Rockster ... Wonder Dog ... who makes every day a good day. And, as we both know, if you apply your nose to the grindstone – whiskery or otherwise – then you have the greatest chance of success you will ever know and the greatest sense of achievement to follow.

Wiser, safer, forever.

Profile: Sherlock, Hydrocarbon Detection Dog

Name: Sherlock
Registered name: Leawyn Logic
Breed: Working Cocker Spaniel

Date of birth: 04/09/2012
Born: Chesterfield, Derbyshire
Sex: Dog

Coat: Black with small amounts of white (mainly on feet and chest with a smudge on his nose)

Kennel Club number: AP03531004

Sherlock was purchased by Clive Gregory on behalf of London Fire Brigade when Sherlock was only ten weeks old. Clive says finding the perfect dog for the job is always a long process, but after searching high and low, he was glad he worked so hard to find Sherlock as he was just what the Brigade was looking for. He showed a natural talent and instinct that Clive couldn't believe.

Dave Arnold, Fire Investigator and Dog Handler (of Sam, the London Fire Brigade's yellow Labrador Fire Dog) was Sherlock's first dad, until Sherlock was nine months old, after which Paul Osborne was selected as the next Dog Handler for the team, and so became Sherlock's partner.

Profile: Paul Osborne, Fire Investigator and Hydrocarbon Detection Dog Handler

Background:

I joined the Fire Service in 1997. I served for my first eight years in the Kent Fire Brigade as a whole-time fire-fighter based at Dartford Fire Station. It was during my time in the Kent Fire Brigade that I started to develop an interest in Fire Investigation. I transferred into the London Fire Brigade in 2005 as it offered greater opportunity for personal development. I had also identified that London had its own dedicated Fire Investigation Team. Kent, like many other brigades in the United Kingdom, has the Fire Investigation role as an additional role for a Station Manager. London's dedicated Investigation team was a real incentive for me to transfer and go for promotion. In London I have served at Southwark, Croydon and Dowgate fire stations as an operational firefighter.

In my career I've been fortunate to spend three years as a Firefighter Development Instructor training recruits in the LFB. This taught me many valuable skills, one of which was how to interact with people to get the most from them. This is something I use lots of when on scene, engaging with a vast range of people from members of the public to members of specialist police teams.

I applied for selection for Fire Investigation in 2009 and was successful in the process. I spent a year and a half training and developing at New Cross in Fire Investigation before returning to Croydon station awaiting a full-time vacancy in the team. In 2012 I became a full-time member of the team, which had centralised to Dowgate Fire Station. In 2013 I was again fortunate in selection to be one of the two Hydrocarbon Dog handlers in the LFB and one of just fourteen teams in the UK. I was paired with Sherlock, who is never far from my side. We graduated from our training at the end of 2013 and have been at the forefront of many high-profile incidents and events throughout London and all over the country ever since. In 2016 we attempted to attend as many station open days celebrating 150 years of the LFB as possible. It was a real honour to meet the public we work so hard for.

The challenges of the role:

The role of a Fire Investigator is a very high-profile one. You are expected to know all the answers in a vast range of different circumstances and be able to educate yourself sometimes at the scene of a fire and then pass on that knowledge to people within or outside our organisation. As firefighters we are known to sometimes be task-focused but to be a good Fire Investigator you need to remove the blinkers (so to speak) and be able to consider anything and everything in order to answer the most important questions of what, when, why, who and how? We attend all the fatal fires that occur in London. Being aware of your own wellbeing and making sure that you utilise the numerous support networks open to us is paramount as the role can be very stressful and upsetting.

You need to be committed to the role and be the type of person that not only identifies a problem but can provide a number of solutions. The commitment not only needs to come from you but from your family too. Those at home need to understand that you will often not finish on time. When you join the team there is a learning curve like no other. I have never worked harder in my career; however, nor have I ever been happier! Being part of a team that has a well-respected voice and valued opinion inside and outside the Brigade is a positive reflection on how hard we have all worked over the years.

The best part of the role:

Being on the front line of duty and putting fires out was enjoyable for me; however, I was always interested in the circumstances of the incidents I attended, and wanted to be able to answer those niggling questions: what, when, why, who and how? As a firefighter I had joined to try and make a positive difference to people's lives. I realised early on in my career that identifying causes of fire and trying to reduce or eliminate them is more positive than picking up the pieces after the fact. Sometimes what is achieved away from incidents, working together with different organisations, can be really valuable in making people's lives, houses and workplaces safer, such as the Total Recalls campaign (www.london-fire.gov.uk/product-recalls.asp). I am proud to have been part of the Fire Investigation team that is bringing about real change.

Interesting incident:

Before becoming a Fire Investigator I thought that spontaneous combustion or self-heating, was something that was so rare it hardly ever happened, if at all ... I have not only been fortunate enough to be on a Fire Investigation training course where this was recreated but have investigated this phenomenon many times. The most recent case was in a fast-food chain in New Malden where oil impregnated into paper towels was left in the kitchen area. After confirming all electrical items in the area of origin weren't the cause and that there had been no human interaction, I started to consider self-heating as a possibility. When I researched the oil that the company used I identified it contained rapeseed oil, which has the ability to self-heat. Following my investigation I recorded the cause of the fire as self-heating. I took time to educate and work with the area manager for the chain so they could make appropriate recommendations regarding the safe disposal of oil-impregnated rags and paper. Our interaction was positive and the company will now be implementing the recommendations.

Acknowledgements

This is my attempt to dip my (metaphorical!) deerstalker hat to those people that enrich my life and have played a part in me being in the fortunate position I find myself of writing my own book. I believe we are all made up from and shaped by so many vast and varied experiences that we have encountered throughout our lives. My life has and continues to be enriched by so many people's warmth and support, and for that I'm lucky, yes ... As well as extremely grateful for their wisdom and guidance in my life. Sadly, some people are no longer with us, but I remember you all with warmth in my heart and take comfort that you rest in peace. I hope that in turn I can inspire others as so many have for me. Not all my friends can be named in this section, but you should all know you make up the rich tapestry of my life and for that I thank you, allowing me to always enjoy the here and now.

So here goes for my acceptance speech! Thank you to:

Isabel George, without whose time (so many hours!), dedication, enthusiasm and belief this wouldn't be possible. Ajda Vucicevic and Becky Millar, my editors at Penguin Random House, this book is testament to your constant encouragement, enthusiasm and unfaltering dedication. And all at Penguin Random House for your behind-the-scenes work on my behalf. I'm only just beginning to realise the heroic efforts and professionalism required to produce a masterpiece!

To all members of 768 Squadron (Hayes School) Air Training Corps, with special mention to Flight Lieutenant Godfrey Smith MBE who believed in me when others didn't, a true friend and brother. Terry Dillon, whose dad was a serving firefighter during the Blitz, your boat trips are a great memory that many will never forget! Chris, Justin and Steve, a band of brothers that can be called upon anytime and anywhere, our trips are part of history! Remember, these are the good old days...

My Kent Fire Brigade colleagues and good friends, the 'Youth Club' of young enthusiastic firefighters I was and am proud to have been part of. My memories of my time with you all will always be happy ones. Special mention to Marc – our sailing excursions and hare-brained trips add another dimension to our friendship, thank you buddy.

To my London Fire Brigade friends of which there are so, so, so many! From Fire Stations to Training Centre, Fire Fighter Development and Fire Investigation, including past, present and future Fire Investigators. We have a responsibility to uphold the very best of the team, to make sure that through our dedication, professionalism, and hours and hours of work behind the scenes, that we do continue to 'Make London a Safer City'. We have, we do and we will continue to achieve this as 'there are no points for second place'! Special mentions to Danielle (Dany) Cotton, you have and continue to be such a positive, inspirational and important figure both inside and outside our organisation; your support of the Fire Investigation Dog Team is invaluable. Charlie Pugsley, your friendship, understanding, belief and support to develop me into what you see I can be. Dave Robinson, your time and support for my family and me; a good manager who knows a solid foundation will provide real results. White Watch Fire Investigation, namely Stu, Owen, Mat and Mark; a dedicated team I'm privileged to serve with and continue to learn from every day. Thank you for supporting Sherlock and me and promoting our work at every turn. To Dave and Lynne, thank you for looking after Sherlock in the early days and being strong enough to say goodbye, I hope I've done you proud. Mick Boyle, words can't convey the admiration I have for you and your work. Your ability to make me think about things in different ways, to achieve real value and results, our training days and working together will always make me smile. Clive Gregory, your dedication to the role of Fire Investigation Dogs in the United Kingdom is firmly in the history books as a huge, huge success. I am so proud to have been trained by you and also to have you as a lifelong friend – I bet you didn't realise how successful you'd be over twenty years ago?! All Fire Investigation Dog Handler teams in the UK, a small elite group I'm proud to be a member of. The LFB team supporting Sherlock and me at this milestone of my career: Marianne Saabye, Michele Rolfe, Christopher Thompson, Leonor Stjepic and Laura Proto. We wouldn't have achieved so much without you doing your very best for us, and for that I thank you. To Pat Rodney, I will never forget your heartfelt support in the early stages when the penny dropped about my dyslexia. To our Counselling and Wellbeing team supporting us and being a solid sounding board, you're all an invaluable asset to the London Fire Brigade, and I know you'd like me to slow down but I just can't!

To Judith and Kelvin at Buckhurst Farm Kennels, thank you for always finding a home for Sherlock, even at last minute! Your five star treatment of Sherlock means I don't worry when I go away. To Debs, thank you for your enthusiasm in supporting the LFB and hours of dog husbandry advice, always such a wealth of information. All at Jack Frost Pet and Country Store, where to start! I am so grateful for the use of your fields for training, advice for dog welfare and always having in stock what I want. Tender Paws Vets, for years of looking after all Sherlock's care, your warmth and compassion. Metropolitan Police Dog Training Establishment, you are world class in all you do. Your support to the LFB is vital and a great example of partnership working at it's best. With special mention to Sean Turner, despite not seeing you as often as I'd like, I know you always do all you can to support our work within the MPS.

To the brother I never had, my oldest friend, Nick Alford, a man who has achieved many amazing things such as swimming the English Channel, who shares my love of wrist watches that we can't afford, and *Top Gun*! 'I feel the need!' To Paul and Louisa, for allowing me to let my hair down over a bottle of wine or two and helping me to forget what I need to forget. To Colin and Pauline, thank you firstly for Kate! And for your love, support and encouragement of us all, you are a huge part of our lives and I'm lucky to have a second set of parents. To my sister Sarah for being one of my biggest fans, you're always with me despite the distance, and I'm very proud to have you and your lovely family in my life. To Mum and Dad, I don't really have enough space for what I'd like to say (it's all good!). Thank you for always believing in me, walking beside me and catching me when I've fallen. For being my heroes, I love you dearly. To Kate, Olivia and Emma, being in your lives completes mine. I could never have achieved so much without your support, understanding and bundles of love. For not complaining when I'm at work, missing Christmases, birthdays or just time together, you are my biggest fans, I'm yours, and I love you.

My last thank you must go to Sherlock! After nearly five years together, who knows how many searches, dog walks and holes have been dug! I have to thank you, my partner in crime! I have all the privilege of working with you, and as I've said countless times before, 'You make me look good!' Thank you for allowing me to be your chauffeur and scribe! Together we have made sure that the Fire Brigade reaches out to a much wider audience than ever before in the communities it serves. We have been a visible presence when needed, and invisible when required to find evidence. Thank you for consistently helping to 'Make London a Safer City', you clever dog!

I have only one question for you buddy... 'When will you calm down?!'

Picture Credits

First plate section
- 'The little crimebuster getting down to work' – © London Fire Commissioner

Second plate section
- 'London Fire Brigade's best and brightest' – © London Fire Commissioner
- '*Daily Mirror* and RSPCA Animal Hero Awards ...' (left) – © Ian West/PA Wire/PA Images
- 'Meeting HRH the Prince of Wales ...' – © Jonathan Brady/PA Archive/PA Images

All other photographs are author's own.

Every reasonable effort has been made to contact all copyright holders, but if there are any errors or omissions, we will insert the appropriate acknowledgement in subsequent printings of this book.